OECD Economic Surveys: Chile 2015

This document and any map included herein are without prejudice to the status of or sovereignty over any territory, to the delimitation of international frontiers and boundaries and to the name of any territory, city or area.

Please cite this publication as:
OECD (2015), *OECD Economic Surveys: Chile 2015*, OECD Publishing, Paris.
http://dx.doi.org/10.1787/eco_surveys-chl-2015-en

ISBN 978-92-64-24843-4 (print)
ISBN 978-92-64-24844-1 (PDF)
ISBN 978-92-64-24845-8 (epub)

Series: OECD Economic Surveys
ISSN 0376-6438 (print)
ISSN 1609-7513 (online)

OECD Economic Surveys: Chile
ISSN 1995-378X (print)
ISSN 1999-0847 (online)

The statistical data for Israel are supplied by and under the responsibility of the relevant Israeli authorities. The use of such data by the OECD is without prejudice to the status of the Golan Heights, East Jerusalem and Israeli settlements in the West Bank under the terms of international law.

Photo credits: Cover © iStockphoto.com/Brent Heit.

Corrigenda to OECD publications may be found on line at: *www.oecd.org/about/publishing/corrigenda.htm*.

Table of contents

Thematic chapters

Tables

Figures

This Survey is published on the responsibility of the Economic and Development Review Committee of the OECD, which is charged with the examination of the economic situation of member countries.

The Economic situation and policies of Chile were reviewed by the Committee on 4 November 2015. The draft was revised in the light of the discussion and given final approval as the agreed report of the whole Committee on 19 November 2015.

The Secretariat's draft report was prepared for the Committee by Sean Dougherty and Eduardo Olaberria, under the supervision of Patrick Lenain. Damien Azzopardi provided statistical research assistance, and Brigitte Beyeler provided administrative support. The Survey also benefitted from contributions from Bert Brys, Martin Fernandez-Sanchez, Guillermo Montt, Ira Postolachi, Diana Toledo Figueroa and Richard Yelland.

The previous Survey of Chile was issued in October 2013.

BASIC STATISTICS OF CHILE, 2014

(Numbers in parentheses refer to the OECD average)*

LAND, PEOPLE AND ELECTORAL CYCLE

Population (million)	17.7		Population density per km²	23.4	(34.9)
Under 15 (%)	21.2	(18.1)	Life expectancy (years, 2013)	78.8	(80.5)
Over 65 (%)	10.0	(16.0)	Men	76.3	(77.8)
Foreign-born (%, 2011)	2.3		Women	81.4	(83.1)
Latest 5-year average growth (%)	0.9	(0.6)	Latest general election	November 2013	

ECONOMY

Gross domestic product (GDP)			Value added shares (%, 2013)		
In current prices (billion USD)	258.2		Primary sector	3.4	(2.6)
In current prices (billion CLP)	147 185		Industry including construction	35.9	(26.5)
Latest 5-year average real growth (%)	4.6	(1.9)	Services	60.6	(71.0)
Per capita (000 USD PPP)	22.4	(39.0)			

GENERAL GOVERNMENT[b]

Per cent of GDP

Expenditure[a]	20.8	(41.9)	Gross financial debt[a]	15.1	(112.6)
Revenue[a]	22.4	(37.8)	Net financial debt[a]	-4.4	(69.5)

EXTERNAL ACCOUNTS

Exchange rate (CLP per USD)	570		Main exports (% of total merchandise exports)	
PPP exchange rate (USA = 1)	371		Crude materials, inedible, except fuels	33.6
In per cent of GDP			Manufactured goods	32.8
Exports of goods and services	33.8	(53.7)	Food and live animals	19.1
Imports of goods and services	32.3	(49.6)	Main imports (% of total merchandise imports)	
Current account balance	-1.1	(0.0)	Machinery and transport equipment	34.2
Net international investment position	-13.8		Mineral fuels, lubricants and related materials	21.2
			Manufactured goods	11.7

LABOUR MARKET, SKILLS AND INNOVATION

Employment rate for 15-64 year-olds (%)	62.2	(65.7)	Unemployment rate, Labour Force Survey (age 15 and over) (%)	6.4	(7.3)
Men	72.8	(73.6)	Youth (age 15-24, %)	16.4	(15.0)
Women	51.7	(57.9)			
Participation rate for 15-64 year-olds (%)	66.6	(71.2)	Tertiary educational attainment 25-64 year-olds (%, 2011)	17.8	(33.3)
Average hours worked per year	1 990	(1 770)	Gross domestic expenditure on R&D (% of GDP, 2013)	0.4	(2.4)

ENVIRONMENT

Total primary energy supply per capita (toe, 2013)	2.2	(4.2)	CO_2 emissions from fuel combustion per capita (tonnes, 2012)	4.5	(9.7)
Renewables (%, 2013)	29.5	(8.8)	Municipal waste per capita (tonnes, 2009)	0.4	(0.5)
Fine particulate matter concentration (urban, PM_{10}, µg/m³, 2011)	60.4	(28.0)			

SOCIETY

Income inequality (Gini coefficient, 2011)	0.503	(0.308)	Ratio of incomes of the top 10% vs. bottom 10%, 2012	26.5	(9.6)
Relative poverty rate (%, 2012)	17.8	(10.9)	Education outcomes (PISA score, 2012)		
Median disposable household income (000 USD PPP, 2011)	8.5	(21.9)	Reading	441	(496)
Public and private spending (% of GDP)			Mathematics	423	(494)
Health care (2013)	7.4	(9.0)	Science	445	(501)
Pensions (2013)	4.4	(8.7)	Share of women in parliament (%, August 2015)	15.8	(26.0)
Education (primary, secondary, post sec. non tertiary, 2011)	3.7	(3.9)			

Better life index: *www.oecdbetterlifeindex.org*

* Where the OECD aggregate is not provided in the source database, a simple OECD average of latest available data is calculated where data exist for at least 29 member countries.

a) 2013 for the OECD aggregate.

b) For Chile, the numbers refer to Central Government.

Source: Calculations based on data extracted from the databases of the following organisations: OECD, International Energy Agency, World Bank, International Monetary Fund, Inter-Parliamentary Union, Central Bank of Chile and Dirección de Presupuestos (DIPRES).

Executive summary

- *Despite sharply lower copper prices, Chile's economic growth has been resilient*
- *Growth needs to become more inclusive, especially for women*
- *School reform is on its way to lift student outcomes*

Despite sharply lower copper prices, Chile's economic growth has been resilient

GDP growth should recover

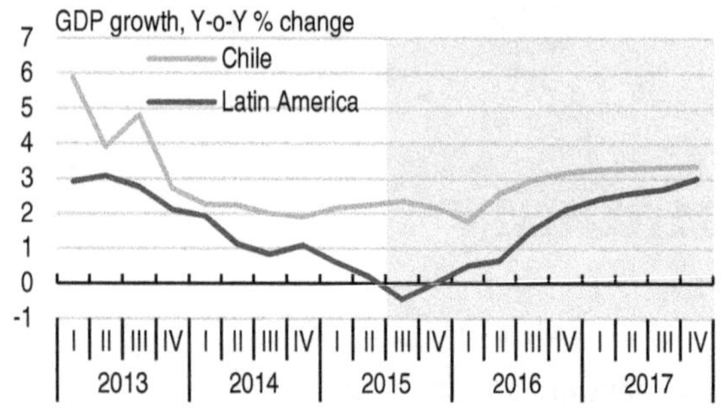

Source: *OECD Economic Outlook 98 database.*

StatLink http://dx.doi.org/10.1787/888933302140

A long period of strong economic growth has improved the well-being of Chileans and reduced poverty dramatically. The sound macroeconomic framework and flexible exchange rate made growth resilient in the face on large commodity price volatility, including the recent fall in copper prices. For growth to remain strong, Chile will need to further expand its economy beyond extracting natural resources, and increase its knowledge-based contribution to global value chains, including by undertaking productivity-enhancing structural reforms.

Growth needs to become more inclusive, especially for women

Participation of women is relatively low

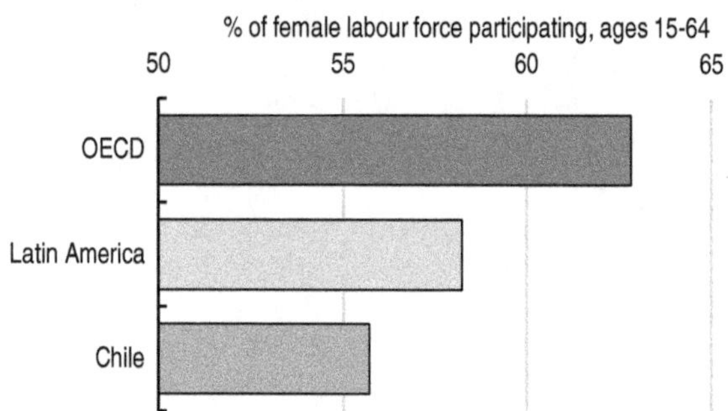

Source: *OECD Employment and Labour Market Statistics 2014.*

StatLink http://dx.doi.org/10.1787/888933302159

Despite strong economic growth, Chile remains a highly unequal society in terms of income, wealth and education. Inequality is passed from one generation to the next, reducing opportunities to climb the social ladder. Chile is now reforming its tax system to make it more progressive and expanding social programmes. Key reforms seek to reduce gender gaps and thus achieve a fairer society. But labour market duality still results in a very unequal wage distribution.

School reform is on its way to lift student outcomes

Many students lack minimum skills

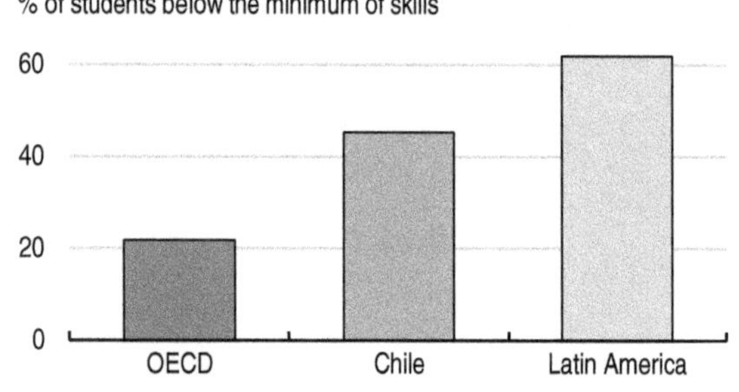

Source: *OECD, PISA 2012 Database.*

StatLink http://dx.doi.org/10.1787/888933302167

School enrolment is high, although the quality of education is uneven, and access to the best schools is reserved primarily for well-off families. Education is being reformed to create better opportunities for the less well-off. Skill mismatches appear high, reflecting education deficiencies that hold back productivity growth. The government's education reform seeks to make schools more inclusive and reshape teacher careers. Efforts are underway to strengthen early childhood education and care, as well as increase the quality of primary, secondary and tertiary education. More investment in vocational education and training will be needed.

MAIN CHALLENGES	KEY RECOMMENDATIONS
Address the high inequality of opportunity	
Persistent limited social mobility and high inequality	Strengthen policies to make growth more inclusive.
Low average levels of educational performance and a high degree of inequity across students	Ensure that schools are more responsive to vulnerable students, especially by boosting the quality of outcomes. Approve the legislation to strengthen teachers' career paths. Link funding for tertiary education to improved quality, especially for the least well-off students.
High labour market duality and weak participation rates of women, youth and minorities	Further expand availability and quality of early childhood education and care. Undertake a skills strategy to assess labour market needs and guide training and education policies. Reduce duality in the labour market between protected indefinite contracts and precarious fixed-term contracts.
Improving the pension system to reduce inequality	Increase the capacity of the pension system to provide better income support of the retired.
Pursue further regulatory and institutional reforms to boost trend productivity growth	
Poor productivity outcomes and slowing trend growth	Fully roll out the Productivity Agenda, to strengthen the capacity of dynamic firms to scale up and carry out innovative activities. Improve stakeholder input into the rule-making process and introduce systematic regulatory impact analysis.
Limited trade integration into global value chains	Further reduce the complexity of administrative procedures for business and simplify sector-specific regulations.
Specific weaknesses in the competition framework	Pass the competition bill that strengthens sanctions for cartels, reform the merger control regime and facilitate market studies.
Preserve resilience and help support sustained growth	
Intensified macroeconomic risks and policy uncertainty in light of medium-term risks	While monetary policy should remain accommodative, fiscal policy should focus on gradual budget consolidation. Simplify the 2014 income tax reform, especially for businesses. Shift the tax base towards real-estate property and environmental damages; review the taxation of natural resources. Accelerate the adoption of Basel III banking regulation.

Assessment and recommendations

- *The economy has been more resilient than its peers*
- *Strengthening the inclusiveness of growth*
- *Boosting productivity and investment*

The quality of life of Chileans has improved significantly over the last few decades, and along several dimensions of well-being it approaches the OECD average, notably jobs and earnings, work-life balance and health (Figure 1, Panel A). The increase in average disposable income and reduction in poverty (Panel B) has been among the most rapid in the OECD, as a consequence of economic reforms, such as trade and investment liberalisation, and the sound macroeconomic policies that have controlled inflation and smoothed economic cycles, reducing uncertainty and encouraging investment. Continued progress will require further

Figure 1. **Incomes have risen and well-being is high in many dimensions**

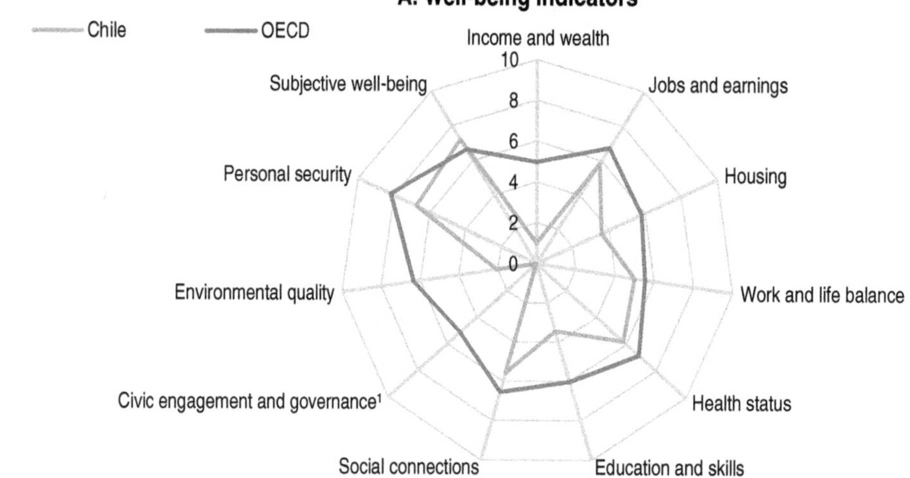

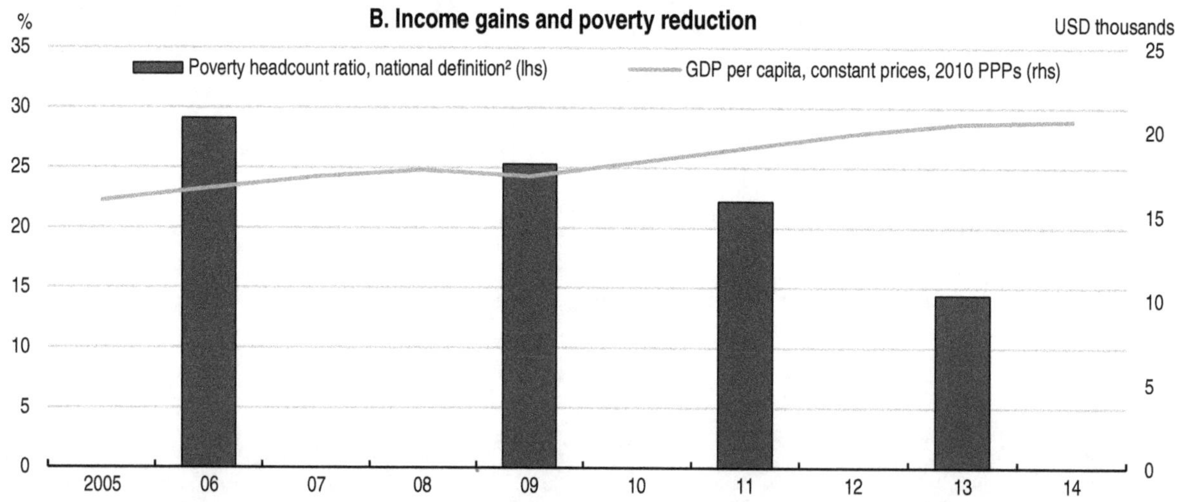

1. The civic engagement and governance dimension is based on: a) consultation in rule-making; and b) voter turnout. Chile has a low score on both measures. However, voter turnout was much higher prior to the latest election, when it was made non-compulsory.
2. The national poverty headcount ratio for a family of four represents a family income below CLP 361 311 per month, in 2013.

Source: OECD, *Well-being Indicators Database*; OECD, *Productivity Database*; and DataStream.

StatLink http://dx.doi.org/10.1787/888933302171

economic transformation towards a more knowledge-based and innovative economy, with more firms capable of participating and upgrading their activities in global value chains. Further improvements in well-being will also need to address the sizable gaps that remain in many well-being indicators across social groups and between sexes (Table 1).

Table 1. **Well-being indicators**

HOW DO MEN AND WOMEN PERFORM IN CHILE?	Chile: Women	Chile: Men	AND IN THE OECD? Women	OECD: Men
Women and men throughout their lifetime				
Health status				
Life expectancy at birth (years)	81	76	83	77
Share of people in good/very good health conditions	51%	67%	67%	72%
Education and skills				
Tertiary degrees awarded (all fields)	57%	43%	58%	42%
Women and men in paid and unpaid work				
Jobs and earnings				
Employment rates (tertiary educated individuals)	71%	87%	79%	88%
Women and men in society				
Civic Engagement and governance				
Share of seats in national parliament	14%	86%	27%	73%
Personal security				
Share of people feeling safe when walking alone at night	49%	60%	61%	79%
Subjective well-being				
Levels of life satisfaction on a 0 to 10 scale	6.6	6.7	6.7	6.6

Source: OECD (2014), How's Life in Chile.

The government has embarked on an ambitious reform agenda to tackle these challenges. The present report reviews and discusses these reforms, in particular:

- In order to make growth more inclusive, reform taxes, childcare, labour rules, and also reduce gender gaps.
- A major revamp of the education system would improve social mobility and boost productivity.
- The ambitious agenda to boost productivity, innovation and growth is welcome.

The economy has been more resilient than its peers

The economy is in the midst of a challenging rebalancing process. As the largest producer of copper in the world, Chile benefited immensely from the upswing in commodity prices and the environment of low international interest rates during the recent commodity supercycle. The commodity price boom induced a macroeconomic cycle through its effect on investment (Fornero et al., 2014). Since mining is very capital intensive, investment grew from approximately 2% of GDP in 2002 to almost 7% of GDP in 2012, generating large spillover effects on other sectors, in particular construction. However, the long phase of increasing commodity prices has reversed: copper prices have weakened, and will likely remain at a lower level in the future. The combination of lower copper prices and higher costs has affected mining profitability, sharply reducing investment (Figure 2). Lower terms of trade have also cut household incomes and reigned in private consumption. As a result, output growth slowed sharply in 2014.

Figure 2. **The fall in copper demand has depressed investment and output growth**

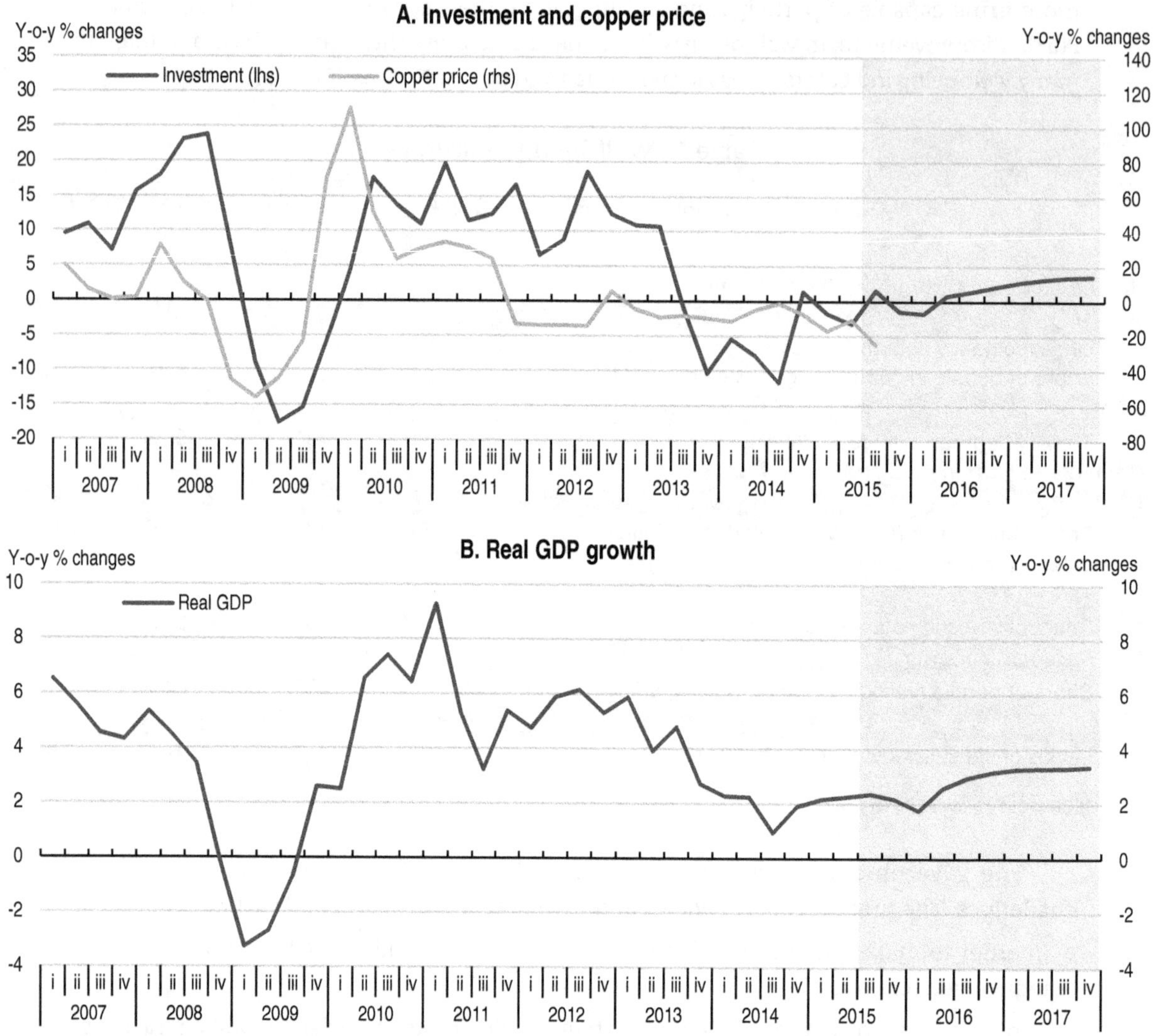

A. Investment and copper price

B. Real GDP growth

Source: Codelco and *OECD Economic Outlook 98 database.*

StatLink http://dx.doi.org/10.1787/888933302186

The large depreciation of the exchange rate has put upward pressure on prices, although inflation expectations remain well-anchored. Inflation rose to 4.7% in 2014, above the Central Bank's tolerance range of 2 to 4%, and has remained high for a number of quarters (Figure 3). The depreciation of the exchange rate has had a significant effect on net exports, mainly through its impact on imports. However the stimulus to exports has been less than expected. This was the result of several factors. First, the depreciation of the peso has been driven in part by the appreciation of the dollar which has affected all currencies, in particular in Latin America, where other currency depreciations have been substantially higher than those of Chile – notably Brazil and Colombia. Second, external demand has weakened, especially in China and Latin America, more than counterbalancing the expansionary effect of the peso depreciation. Finally, the exchange rate elasticity of industrial exports has likely declined over time, in part as a result of the further integration of trade linkages (Ahmed et al., 2015).

Figure 3. **Depreciation has put upward pressure on prices**

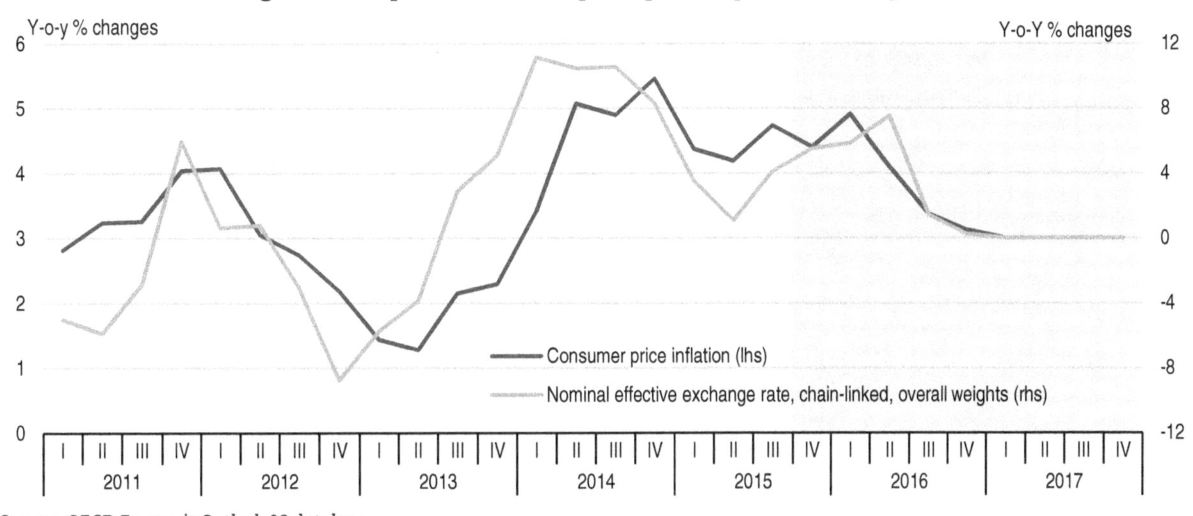

Source: OECD Economic Outlook 98 database.

StatLink http://dx.doi.org/10.1787/888933302195

With headline inflation exceeding the policy target, the central bank raised interest rates from 3% to 3.25% in mid-October 2015. However, given the downside risks to the recovery and well-anchored inflation expectations, monetary policy can remain accommodative. Raising interest rates further in the near term may not be necessary, because recent inflation has been mainly associated with exchange rate depreciation, which the rebalancing process needs, and is not linked with supply-side pressures. Indeed, the weakening local and external activity and recent decrease in commodity prices suggest that pressure on prices should diminish. But if expectations persistently exceed the target, some further monetary tightening may be warranted.

Despite the substantial slowdown of output and domestic demand, unemployment has remained relatively stable at low levels (Figure 4). Annual wage growth accelerated, reaching a relatively high rate, but has begun to decline. This apparent discrepancy between relatively weak output and strong labour market performance has generated some degree of concern, to the extent that it could be an indication that the economy's spare capacity is smaller than widely thought, and therefore, that high inflation may be more persistent than projected.

A fiscal impulse to the economy has taken place in 2015, mainly via automatic stabilisers, which are allowed to operate freely according to Chile's fiscal rule. Central government spending has increased by 8.4% from last year, mainly funded by tax increases. The authorities feel that fiscal consolidation is warranted to adjust to the permanent negative shock income shock generated by lower copper prices. However, this consolidation should be carried out gradually to smooth its social impact, and adjusted if necessary in light of the pace of recovery. The 2016 budget foresees an increase in expenditure of 4.4%, only half the growth of 2015.

The recent slowdown in activity and currency depreciation have had little impact on the balance sheets of corporations, thanks in part to limited currency mismatch (Central Bank of Chile, 2015a). Some bank payment indicators have deteriorated, most notably medium-sized ones, but in general, bank financial indicators are stable (see Table 3 below) and stress tests suggest that capital levels are sufficient to confront a severe stress

Figure 4. **Unemployment has remained low but is rising**

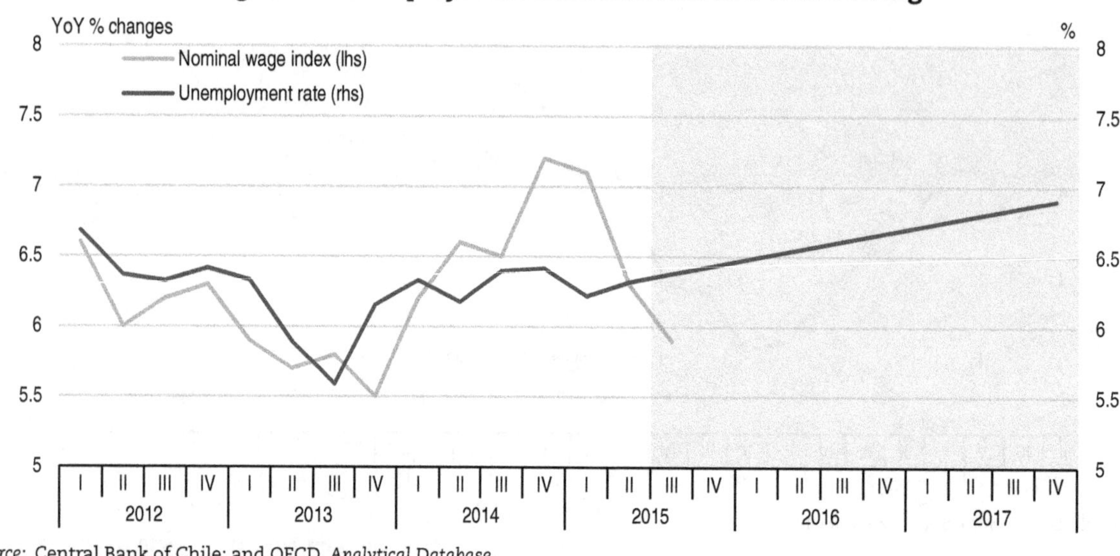

Source: Central Bank of Chile; and OECD, *Analytical Database*.

StatLink http://dx.doi.org/10.1787/888933302209

scenario. Bond issues by the banks contributed to the diversification of funding sources, although medium-sized banks are highly dependent on wholesale funding. Finally, the high levels of capitalisation could weather the materialisation of a severe stress scenario.

Output is expected to grow by 2.2% in 2015, sustained by a fiscal impulse, and accelerate to 2.6% in 2016 and 3.3% in 2017, as private domestic demand gradually strengthens (Table 2). Exchange rate depreciation will likely induce a substantial growth in exporting activities. A significant number of workers may move from mining to other sectors that gain in competitiveness. Many workers may need retraining, and, very likely, relocation from mining regions to other locations.

Chile faces several medium-term uncertainties

Chile faces potential medium-term uncertainties from external and internal sources. The most substantial is probably a larger-than-expected slowdown in China, destination of one-quarter of Chile's exports (Figure 5), about 80% of which are copper-related. Simulations by the OECD suggest that a two percentage point reduction in the growth rate of domestic demand in China would result in a one-half percentage point reduction in Chile's GDP growth. Knock-on effects could make this even larger. Brazil remaining in the current deep recession also poses an important demand risk, given its important regional role. Further shocks that Chile could face include those from copper prices, the inevitable rise in interest rates by the US Federal Reserve, and the consequences of natural disasters. Most of these shocks could have strong negative consequences (Box 1).

The fiscal rule has worked well but could be made more robust

The fiscal rule helped Chile to run current account surpluses during much of the commodity boom. Fiscal surplus rose from 2% in 2004 to over 7% of GDP in 2007, allowing the country to save more than 10% of GDP in its sovereign wealth funds. Then the surpluses switched to deficits as a result of the countercyclical response to the 2009 global financial crisis, reconstruction spending related to the 2010 earthquake and tsunami, and the increase in production costs in mining and the internalisation of what then seemed to

Table 2. **Macroeconomic indicators and projections**
Percentage changes, constant prices

	2012 Current prices (billion CLP)	2013	2014	2015	2016	2017
GDP	129 028	**4.3**	**1.8**	**2.2**	**2.6**	**3.3**
Private consumption	80 665	5.9	2.2	1.8	2.8	3.4
Government consumption	15 674	3.4	4.4	4.2	3.9	2.6
Gross fixed capital formation	31 044	2.1	-6.1	-1.3	0.7	3.3
Housing	4 260	-1.4	1.7	2.2	2.6	3.3
Final domestic demand	127 383	4.6	0.5	1.4	2.5	3.2
Stockbuilding[1]	1 900	-0.9	-1.1	0.4	-0.5	0.0
Total domestic demand	129 284	3.9	-0.5	2.0	2.0	3.3
Exports of goods and services	44 266	3.4	0.7	-2.6	1.7	4.0
Imports of goods and services	44 522	1.7	-7.0	-3.3	1.9	3.9
Net exports[1]	-256	0.6	2.5	0.2	0.0	0.1
Other indicators (growth rates, unless specified)						
Potential GDP	-	3.9	3.4	3.1	2.9	2.8
Output gap[2]	-	0.5	-1.1	-1.9	-2.2	-1.7
Employment	-	2.1	1.5	1.3	0.9	0.7
Unemployment rate	-	6.0	6.3	6.3	6.6	6.8
GDP deflator	-	1.8	5.5	5.1	3.6	3.5
Consumer price index	-	1.8	4.7	4.4	3.9	3.0
Core consumer prices	-	1.2	3.9	4.6	3.5	2.8
Household saving ratio, net[3]	-	9.8	8.3	7.3	6.5	5.9
Current account balance[4]	-	-3.6	-1.1	0.2	-0.2	-0.1
Terms of trade	-	-3.0	-1.4	0.5	-0.9	0.0
Central government financial balance[4]	-	-0.6	-1.8	–2.9	-2.5	-1.2
Central government gross debt[4]	-	12.8	15.1	..	..	..
Central government net assets (only treasury assets)[4, 5]	-	-1.9	-3.0	..	..	..
Central government net assets (all financial assets)[4, 6]	-	5.7	4.4	..	..	..
Three-month money market rate, average	-	4.9	3.7	3.0	3.6	3.9
Ten-year government bond yield, average	-	5.3	4.7	4.4	4.9	5.0

1. Contribution to changes in real GDP.
2. As a percentage of potential GDP.
3. As a percentage of household disposable income.
4. As a percentage of GDP. Only central government data is available.
5. Only includes treasury assets (ESSF, PRF, Education fund and other treasury assets).
6. Includes treasury assets and other government financial assets (cash, temporary investment and other claims).

Source: OECD Economic Outlook 98 database, and Dirección de Presupuestos (DIPRES).

be permanently higher commodity prices (Figure 6). Nevertheless, the fiscal situation remains robust – notably by the near absence of net debt – which gave the government some room to act counter-cyclically and sustain aggregate demand in response to the 2014 slowdown in activity.

The public financial management framework is robust, but could be enhanced to improve transparency and accountability. For instance, the government's public finance reports describe short-term and long-term fiscal policy, including contingent liabilities and growth and spending assumptions, which have proven useful to assess the fiscal stance. But to provide more predictability, medium-term budget targets could be embedded in the rule itself and be consistent with maintaining a strong government net financial position.

Figure 5. **Export destinations for Chile**

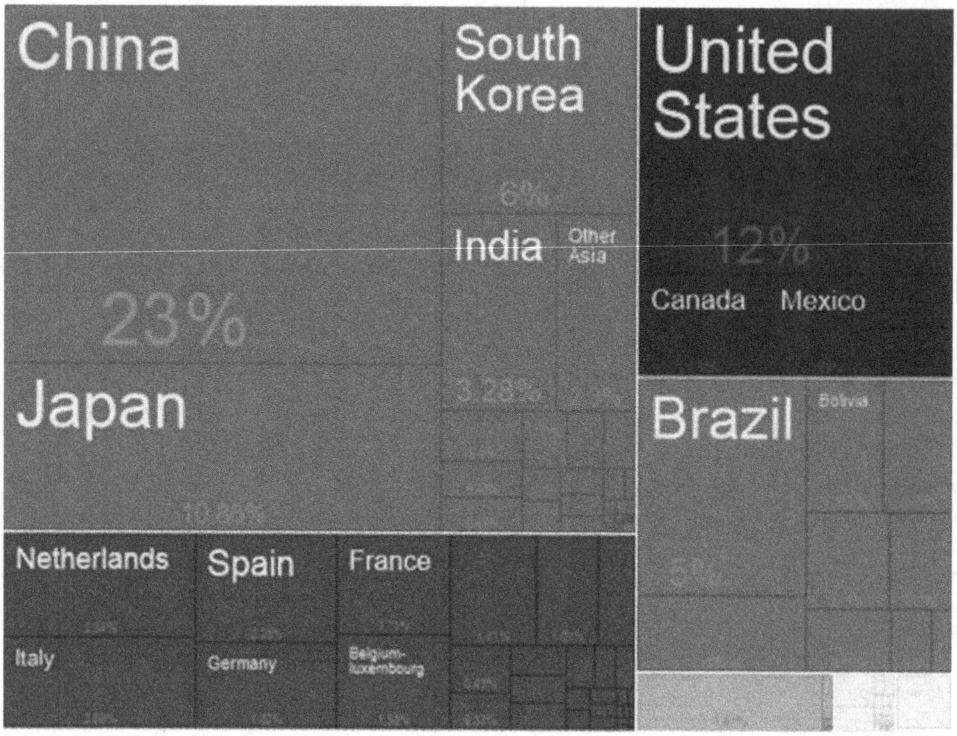

Source: Central Bank of Chile; MIT Observatory on Economic Complexity.

Box 1. Shocks that could affect the Chilean economy

Potential shock	Possible outcome
Copper prices recover or fall further	Chile produces about one-third of the World's copper. Copper represents about half of Chile's exports. Copper prices are now at a level not seen since the financial crisis, due to weak demand. China is the leading importer of copper. Weaker-than-expected GDP growth in China would hurt prices further, while stronger performance could lead to an upswing in prices. Price rises could yield large gains in the terms-of-trade as well as trigger investment, while a further fall in copper prices would weigh on public finances, leaving little margin for supporting domestic demand. Changes in the composition of China's growth may also affect demand for copper, as the economy moves towards more consumption and less investment-led growth.
Volatility following Fed rate increases	As a small open economy with a substantial stock of portfolio flows, Chile is highly exposed to capital outflows, notably corporate non-financial corporations. Uncertainty in the pace of interest rate hikes in the United States and herd behavior could trigger high volatility that could heighten investor uncertainty, hindering the recovery.
Natural disasters	Chile is unusually exposed to natural disasters, including earthquakes, floods and fires. While economic damage was highly limited in the September 2015 earthquake, during the previous earthquake in 2010, Chile experienced a 17% loss of capital, as a share of GDP, and required considerable subsequent rebuilding.

The Fiscal Advisory Council was created in 2012 – a welcome step, but its institutional design could be strengthened in accordance with best practices. Greater autonomy for the Council should be built in a fiscal responsibility law to ensure independent assessment of compliance with the fiscal rules in the future.

Figure 6. **The government's fiscal and financial positions remain sound**

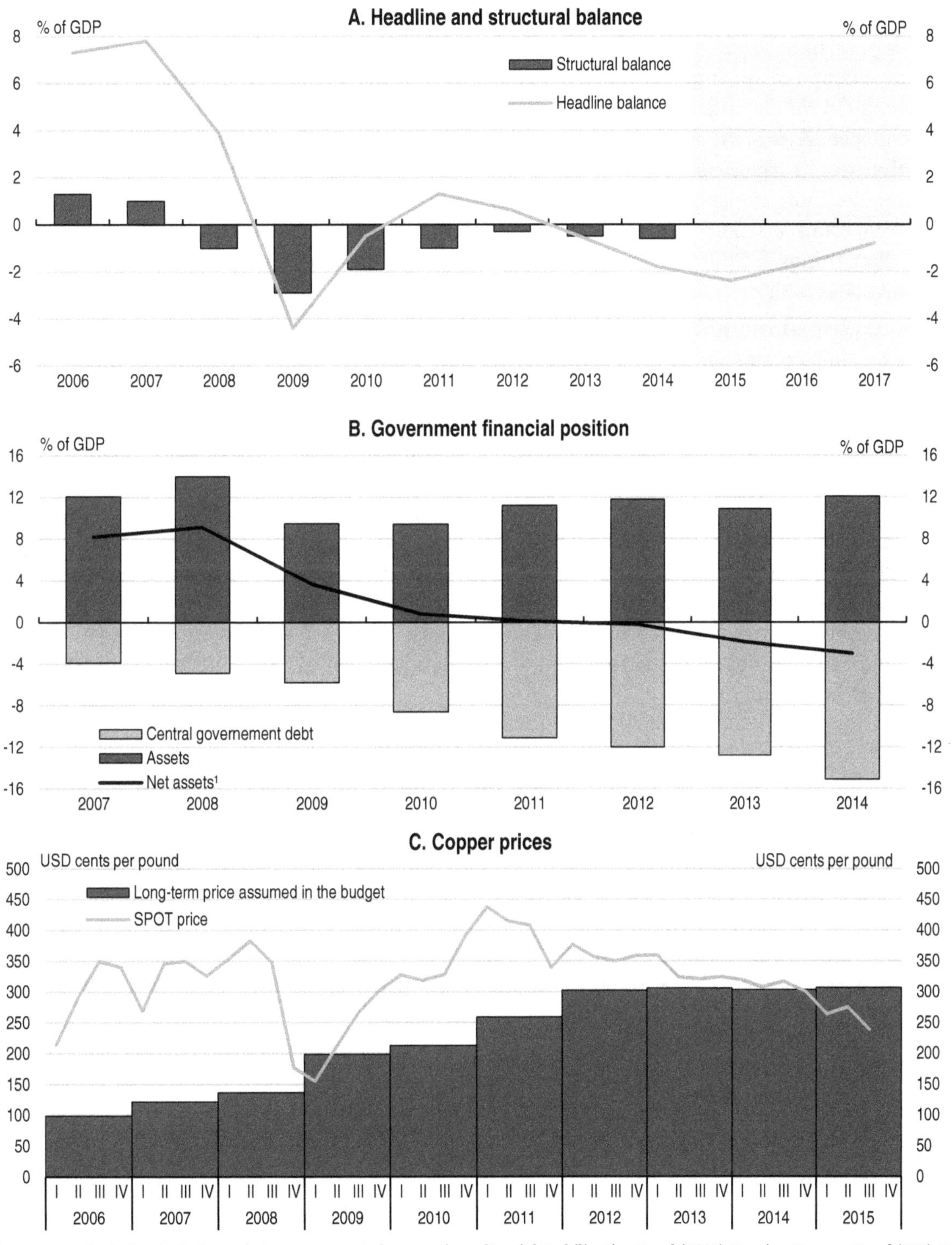

1. Net assets calculation includes only treasury assets [Economic and Social Stabilization Fund (ESSF), Pension Reserve Fund (PRF), Fund for Education (FpE) and other treasury assets].

Source: Central Bank of Chile, Ministry of Finance and Chilean Copper Commission, Ministry of Mining.

StatLink http://dx.doi.org/10.1787/888933302221

Banking supervision could be further strengthened

The government must continue to modernise the institutional framework of financial supervision. Today, the superintendents of banks and securities are selected by the president and appointed at the beginning of each presidential term, with no justification required for dismissal. The government has submitted a bill to Congress to enhance the independence of the securities and insurance regulator (SVS) by establishing a commission that would include some members with terms independent of the political cycle and require more transparent justification for dismissal. The government has also publicly compromised sending a new Banking Law to Congress before the end of 2015 that, among other things, will grant more independence to the banking and financial institution regulator (SBIF).

Furthermore, unlike other emerging economies which are already implementing the Basel III recommendations on bank capital, Chile has yet to define a timeline or make an implementation plan. The government is expected to send a new Banking Law to Congress before the end of 2015, which will adapt Basel III recommendations to the Chilean case. It is important that these recommendations are implemented to avoid major regulatory discrepancies between domestic and foreign banks, considering that the parent companies of European banks operating in Chile are already implementing Basel III. The changes should be implemented gradually, taking into account the cyclical position of the economy. Although non-performing loans (NPLs) are generally not a problem (average NPL ratio of around 2%), and banks are generally well-capitalised (core equity ratio of around 10%), it is nonetheless expected that some banks would fall short of the Basel III standards regarding total capital ratios (Table 3). However, a more detailed analysis at the level of individual banks is needed.

Table 3. **Financial indicators**

% unless otherwise stated

	2010	2011	2012	2013	2014
Consolidated banking system					
Credit growth (real annual change)	5.1	12.9	11.6	11.0	4.8
Mortgage credit growth (real annual change)	9.0	8.1	8.9	10.2	10.3
NPL ratio (non-performing loans/total loans)	2.7	2.4	2.2	2.1	2.2
Provisions (provisions/total loans)	2.5	2.3	2.3	2.4	2.4
Capital adequacy (regulatory capital/risk-weighted assets)	14.1	13.9	13.3	13.3	13.4
Return on equity (ROE)	18.6	17.4	14.5	14.9	17.2
Corporate and household sector					
Corporate indebtedness (% GDP)	84.2	89.1	94.7	102.1	109.6
Household indebtedness (% Income)	57.3	55.9	54.7	57.1	60.8
External sector					
Gross external debt (% GDP)	35.9	42.7	44.7	50.7	60.1
External debt (foreign liabilities/assets)	8.2	9.3	8.0	8.8	8.8
International reserves (millions USD)	27 864	41 979	41 650	41 094	40 447

Source: Central Bank of Chile.

Non-financial corporate and household debt has increased, driving the debt-to-GDP ratio of non-financial firms to around 100% in 2014. This level is higher than that of other emerging economies but still lower than many OECD countries. Household debt also rose to about 60% of disposable income in 2014, driven by higher mortgage debt. This could be in part a result of households bringing forward their home purchasing in anticipation of the scheduled increase in VAT on housing from 2016. Despite higher debt, household debt service-to-income ratios have remained at low level due to low interest rates. In the case of mortgages, loan-to-value ratios have been declining (Central Bank of Chile, 2015b).

The increase in to non-Financial corporate debt does not necessarily imply a significant risk to financial stability thanks to a series of mitigating factors. First, rollover risks seem moderate, as the average time to maturity of outstanding debt is around 15 years. Second, the increased reliance on foreign currency funding does not seem to be associated with greater currency mismatches. Third, firms with large net foreign currency liabilities are usually associated with significant natural hedges. Finally, a large portion of this foreign currency debt is FDI related, which is typically less sensitive to external financial shocks.

Recalibrating some aspects of the reform agenda could contribute to raising business confidence

Addressing the recent loss of business confidence will be important to aid in the return to stronger growth (Figure 7). Although the decrease in confidence is mainly explained by lower commodity prices and the normalisation of US monetary policy, it also reflects some uncertainty in the business community about certain aspects of the government's reform agenda, including the tax reform in particular, which has been seen as further complicating the corporate tax system. The administration has sought to temper this uncertainty in several dimensions. In the case of the tax reform, it is defining more clearly who needs to follow which accounting rules under the new hybrid tax system.

Figure 7. **Consumer and business confidence has deteriorated**

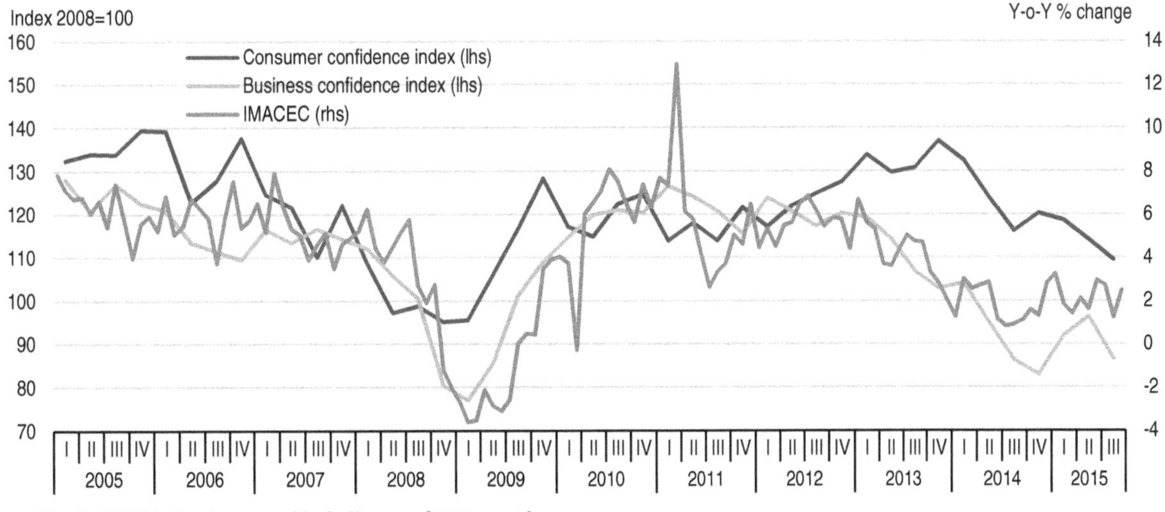

Note: The IMACEC index is a monthly indicator of GDP growth.
Sources: Central Bank of Chile, National Statistics Institute (NSI) and Universidad Adolfo Ibañez/ICARE.

StatLink http://dx.doi.org/10.1787/888933302239

Strengthening the inclusiveness of growth

Stronger economic growth in Chile needs to be complemented by a reduction in inequality in order to make the gains more inclusive. Although poverty has been reduced dramatically, inequality as measured by the Gini after taxes and transfers remains the highest in the OECD (Figure 8). Even after including estimated in-kind transfers from education and health, a large gap remains with other countries. The current Chilean

Figure 8. **Social cohesion indicators**

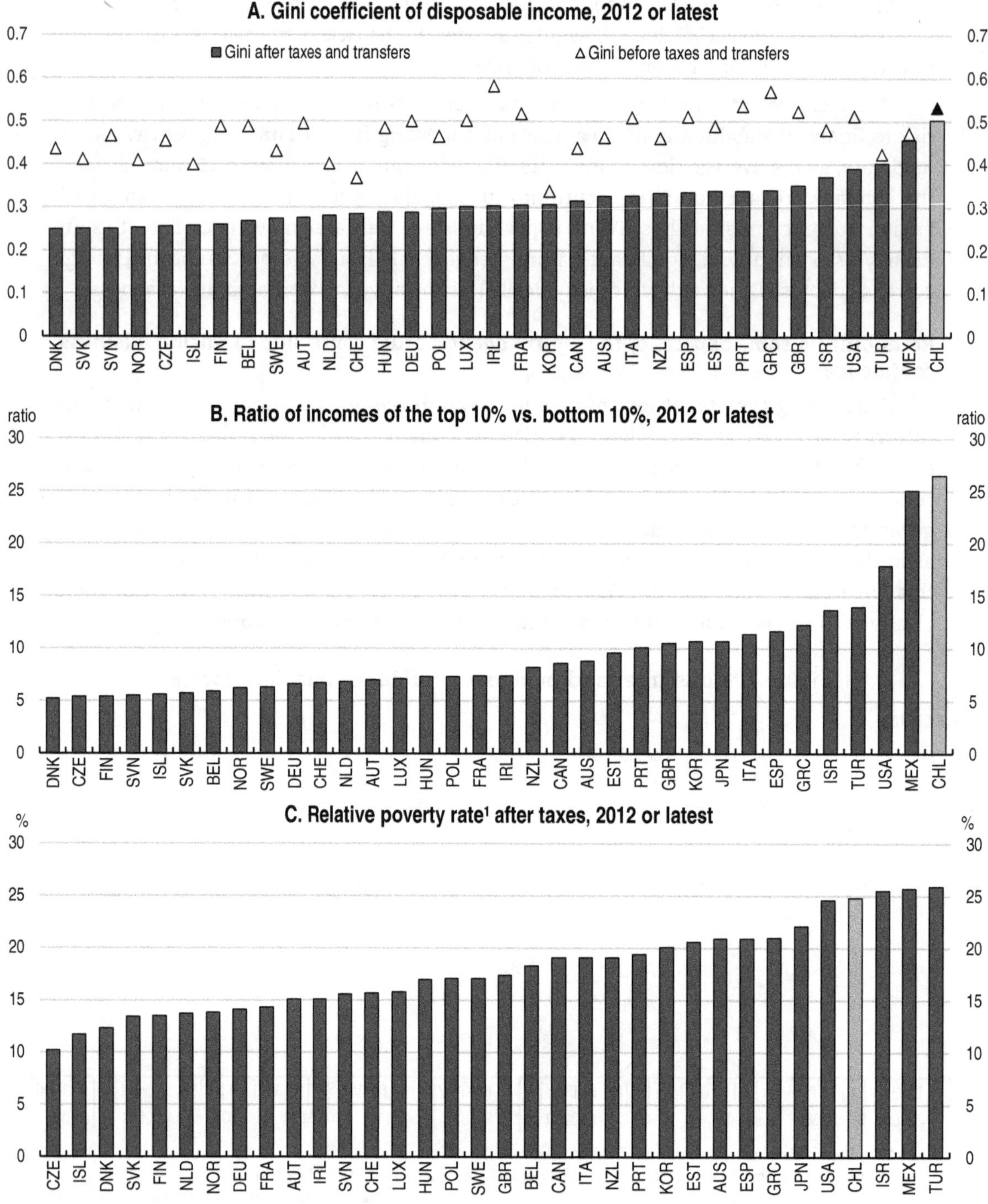

1. The poverty rate is the percentage of households who fall below the poverty line which is set at 60% of median household income.
Source: OECD Better Life Index and OECD, *Income Distribution and Poverty Database*.

StatLink http://dx.doi.org/10.1787/888933302249

administration has adopted an ambitious policy agenda to tackle inequality. This includes a tax reform to raise more revenue and expand social programmes; a labour reform to promote a more inclusive labour market; and an education reform to build more inclusive schools and reduce skill gaps across socio-economic groups.

Better quality and equity of compulsory education is the linchpin of inclusive growth

Education and skills development can play a key role in reducing income inequality and increasing growth. The inability of individuals from poor socio-economic backgrounds to access higher education and develop their human capital causes income inequality to perpetuate over time, lowering economic growth (Causa and Johansson, 2010). In the long run, education has among the largest effects on economic growth (Barnes et al., 2011; OECD, 2015a). Evidence shows that growth is directly and significantly related to the skills of the population (Hanushek and Woessmann, 2015), and with collective cognitive skills is by far the most important determinant of a country's economic growth (Figure 9).

Figure 9. **Better quality of education increases economic growth**

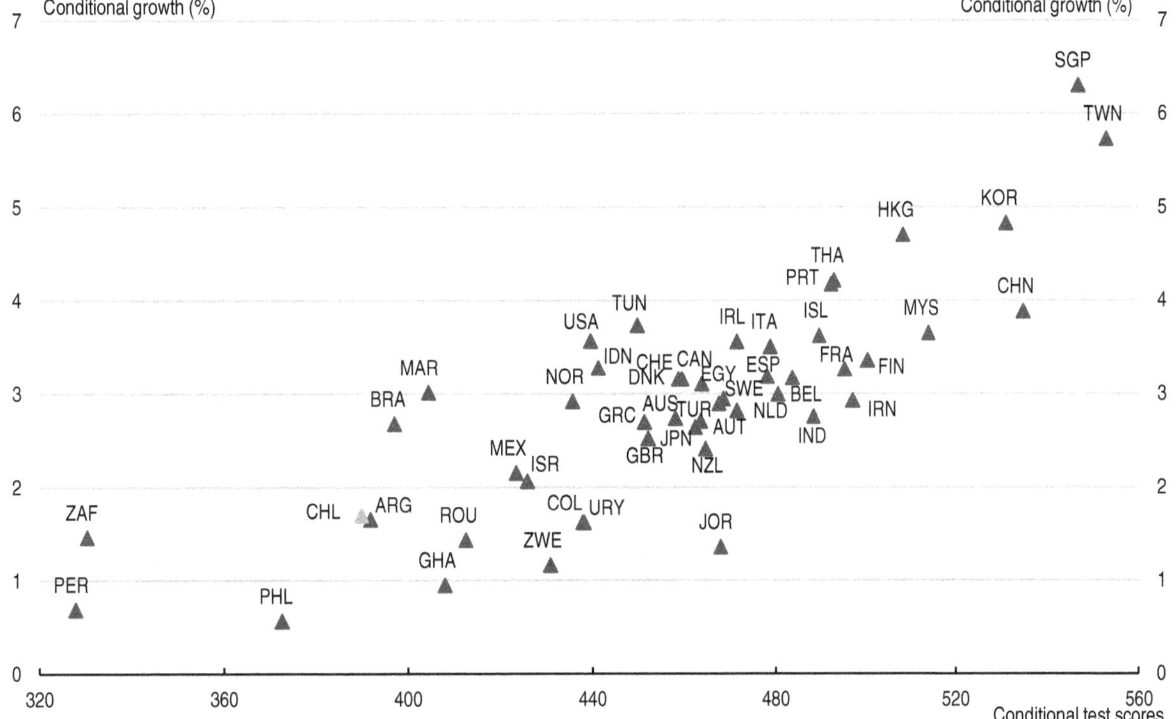

Source: OECD (2015i), *Universal Basic Skills: What Countries Stand to Gain.*

How to read this figure: This figure depicts the fundamental association between annual growth in real per capita GDP between 1960 and 2000 and average test scores, after controlling for differences in initial per capita GDP and initial average years of schooling. Countries align closely along the regression line that depicts the positive association between cognitive skills and economic growth.

StatLink http://dx.doi.org/10.1787/888933302251

In Chile, despite significant progress over the last decades attracting more students to the education system, performance remains below most OECD countries (Chapter 2). The average student in Chile has a PISA score in reading, math and science that is much lower than the OECD average and one of the lowest in the OECD. And the average difference in results, between the students with the highest socio-economic background and the students with the lowest socio-economic background, is also significantly higher than the OECD average. Chile also has a significant proportion of young people that are unable to fully attain basic skills in PISA exams (420 points on the PISA mathematics scale), which is assumed to represent the minimum skills necessary for participating productively in modern economies (Figure 10).

Figure 10. **Improving education quality to achieve universal basic skills can boost growth of GDP**

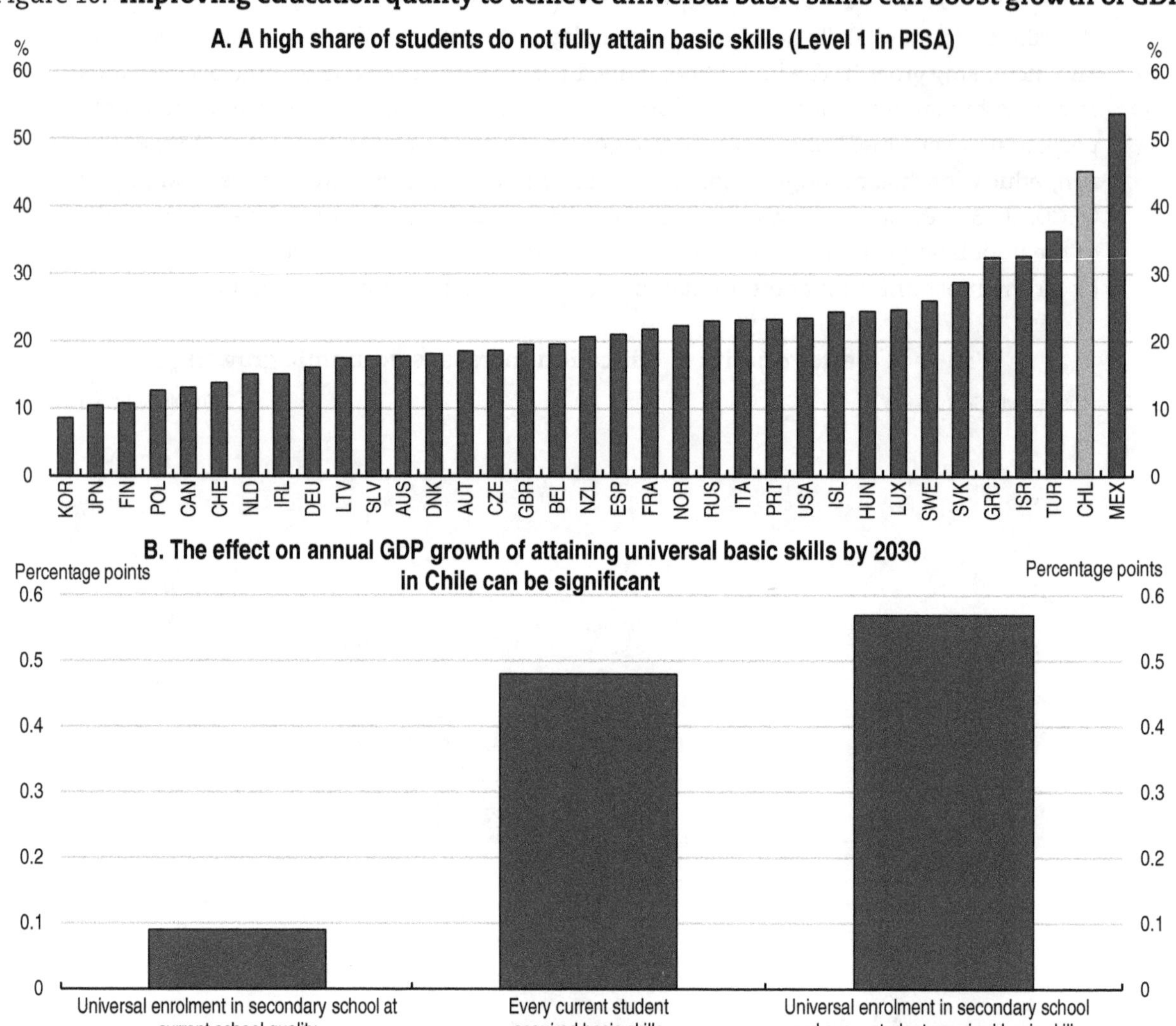

Note: The bars in Panel B refer to annual growth rates (in percentage points) once the whole labour force has reached the specific goal.
Source: OECD, *PISA 2012 Database* and OECD (2015i).

StatLink http://dx.doi.org/10.1787/888933302267

The potential gains of attaining universal skills – all students fully attaining 420 points in the PISA mathematics scale – can be very large. As discussed in Chapter 2, OECD estimates suggest that while ensuring universal schooling at the current level of quality yields small economic gains, improving quality of schools so that each of the current students attains basic skills by 2030 can have a much stronger impact on the economy, In particular, Chile's annual economic growth can increase by 0.48 percentage points per year (an increase of 7% in real GDP by 2030). And if the two previous scenarios are combined, the increase in the annual growth rate of GDP would be 0.57 percentage points (which means that real GDP will be 8½ per cent higher by 2030). Furthermore, achieving universal basic skills has a complementary impact on reducing inequality (OECD, 2015i).

To attain universal basic skills, Chile could benefit from a comprehensive and consistent Skills Strategy. This strategy must begin with a focus on the early years is crucial in addressing socio-economic differences. Early learning confers value on acquired skills, which leads to self-reinforcing motivation to learn more (Heckman, 2013). Indeed, Chile's government has assigned special priority to expanding the coverage of quality services for early childhood. To this end, a law making kindergarten universal was enacted in 2013, and the government has made expanding early childhood education a high priority. The *Nueva institucionalidad de la Educación Parvularia* aims to increase the coverage of preschool education throughout Chile, and to improve and monitor quality through the creation of a Secretariat for Childhood Education and a division for preschool education at the education superintendency. The government created, in a first stage, over 500 new day care facilities across the country. This provides more than 10 000 children between zero and two years old with access to early childcare and education. Furthermore, in the next four years, more than 3 000 day care facilities are to be created, which should bring Chile closer to the OECD in terms of coverage.

A second pillar of the skills strategy should be to build more inclusive schools and improve their quality. The school voucher system that was introduced in 1981 allowed school choice among students, including for attending private schools. This triggered 1 000 private schools to enter the market and boosted the private enrolment rate by 20 percentage points. Empirical evidence shows that this policy led to increased sorting between students and schools and less improvement in terms of quality, partially because schools were allowed to choose students (Hsieh and Urquiola, 2006). As a result, students from lower socio-economic background are disproportionally placed in schools that perform poorly, widening inequities. In contrast, when schools cannot select students based upon their ability, strong competition between them encourages entry by high productivity schools and improves the average skill levels of students (MacLeod and Urquiola, 2009). To address practices that hinder equity and also target low-performing schools and disadvantaged students, the administration proposed and Congress has passed the Inclusion and Equity Law, which aims to stop selection of students by (public and private) subsidised schools, disallow for-profit schools, and eliminate co-payments.

To improve quality Chile also needs to set funding mechanisms that respond to the students' and schools' needs. The level of education spending in Chile at 6.9% of GDP is slightly above the OECD average level of 6.1%. However, spending per student is much lower, at around USD 32 250 (Figure 11). Empirical evidence shows that below around USD 50 000 (at PPP), higher spending per student is associated with better performance, suggesting that increasing spending may improve educational quality (OECD, 2015i). Funding across schools is highly uneven, and often tied to local taxes. Chile needs to develop a better methodology for funding schools, so that it focuses on those that have the greatest needs. The Inclusion and Equity Law increased funds for vulnerable students (using a differentiated voucher called *Subvención Escolar Preferencial*), and extended this voucher to middle class students. This positive development is reinforced by the recent implementation of a new institution responsible for auditing and supervising school providers (*Superintendencia de Educación*).

Finally, to improve the quality of compulsory education Chile needs to strengthen the teaching profession by better defining what teachers can expect as professionals throughout their careers, and providing adequate conditions that allow and motivate teachers to improve. The country currently has a large shortage of qualified teachers, particularly in rural schools, public schools and in schools that receive students from disadvantaged backgrounds. In this regard, a bill was introduced to Congress in 2015 that would reform new teacher certification requirements, and introduce a teacher evaluation process, a salary scale and clarified teacher workloads. It also raises the requirements to enter teaching and heightens demands on educational institutions, to ensure that graduates have the

Figure 11. **Average spending per student between the ages of 6 and 15 is low**

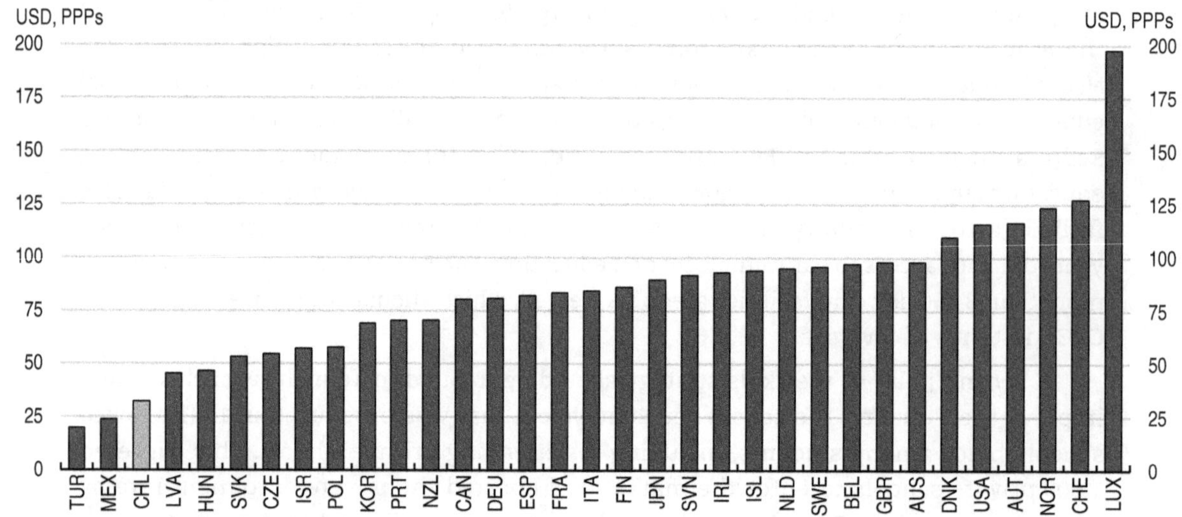

1. Spending is measured in USD PPPs in the year 2012.
Source: OECD, *Education at a Glance Database.*

StatLink http://dx.doi.org/10.1787/888933302278

knowledge and skills to teach, significantly increasing compensation early in teaching careers, even above the average of the salaries of other university graduates, and further increasing as one moves up the salary scale through certification, and provides mentoring to young teachers. These important reforms are discussed further in Chapter 2.

Tertiary education reform should focus on access and quality

To promote equity and increase productivity further, the tertiary education system must be accessible to good students from low income and disadvantaged groups, and quality needs to be improved. In recent decades Chile has made significant progress to expand access to tertiary education. However, since the gap between enrolment among the top and bottom income quintiles remain large, efforts need to be enhanced to ensure that students from low socio-economic background can access tertiary education. Moreover, public funding needs to be linked to positive evaluation of quality, to ensure that enrolment translates into better career prospects. Without such actions, the cycle of inequality will perpetuate over time as there is a strong correlation between tertiary education attainment and socio-economic family background in Chile (Figure 12).

For socio-economically disadvantaged youth, better measures to remove financial barriers to undertaking higher education are required. Across OECD countries, the most common approach is public funding through direct loans. An alternative, which has been used in Chile, is private funding leveraged by the government. In 2012, the government started subsidising interest rates and making repayment income-contingent. To reduce financial constraints to students from lower income families, the government is considering providing free higher education, from 2016, to all students from families that are in the bottom half of the income distribution, that are enrolled in institutions that fulfil some quality and governance requirements. This would certainly help reduce financial constraints to access tertiary education for many students from middle and lower income families. However, this policy will be very costly and will likely not guarantee that lower income students will be able to access and graduate from tertiary education.

Figure 12. **Access to tertiary education has improved but remains unequal**

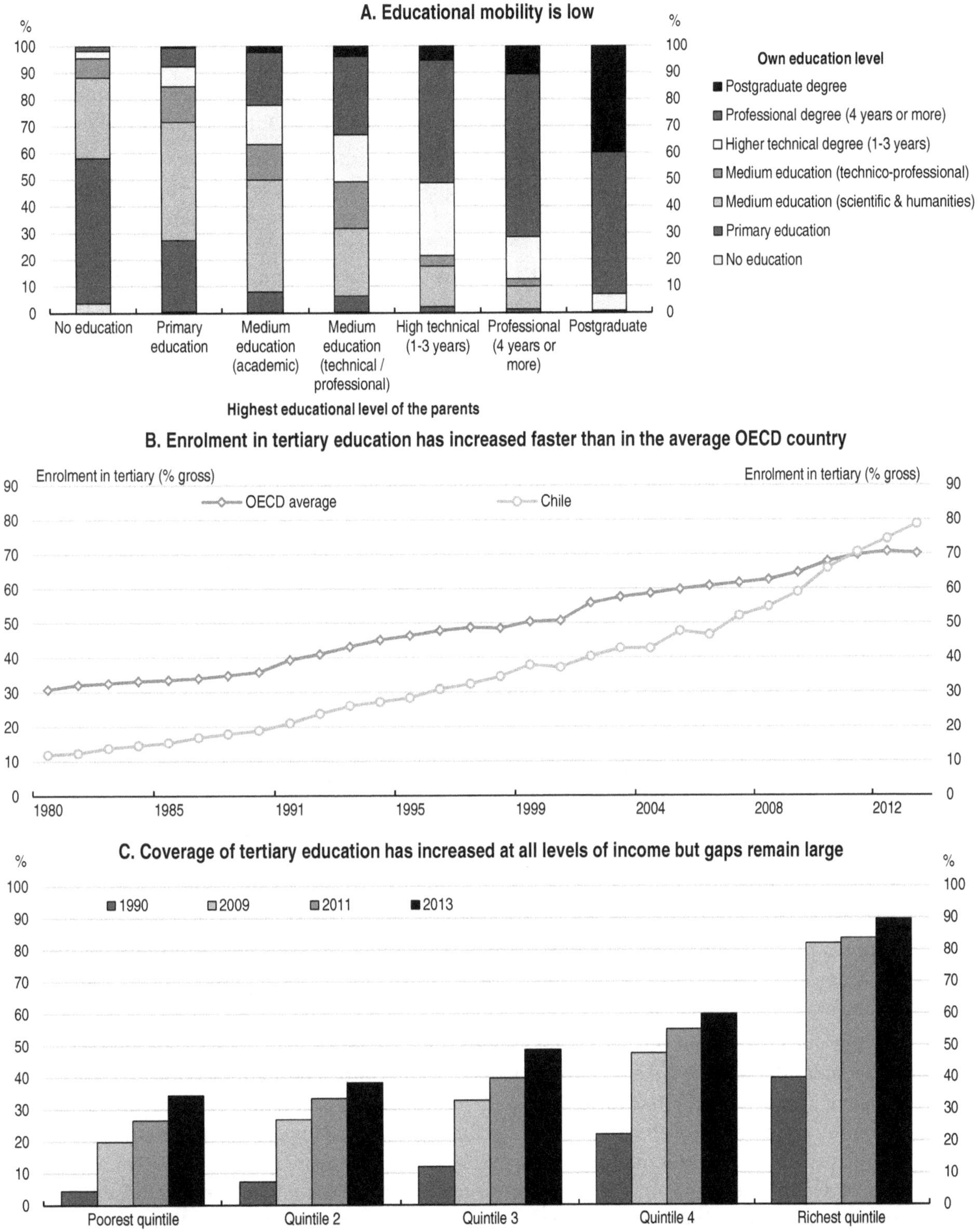

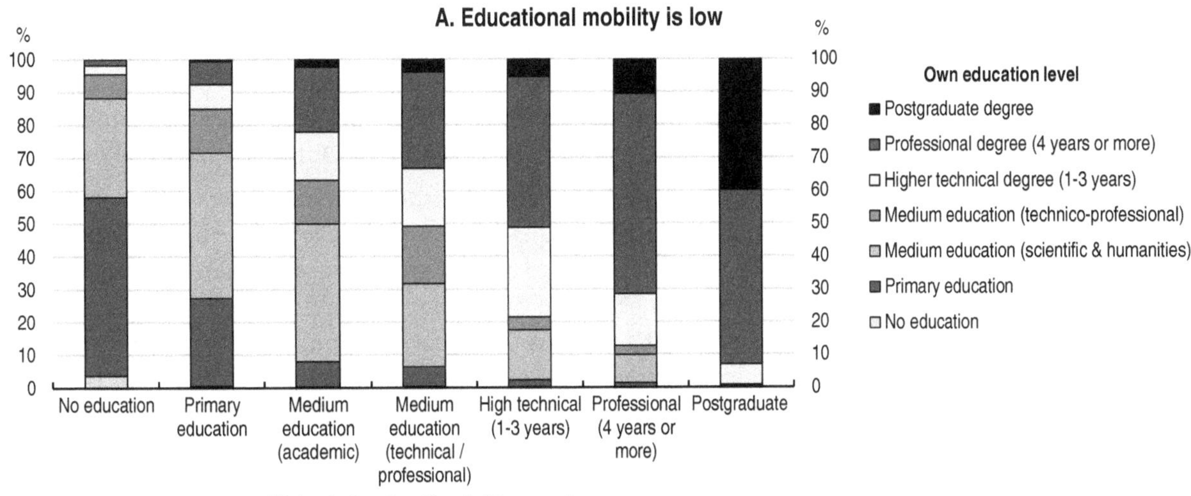

B. Enrolment in tertiary education has increased faster than in the average OECD country

Enrolment in tertiary (% gross)

OECD average

Chile

1980 1985 1991 1995 1999 2004 2008 2012

C. Coverage of tertiary education has increased at all levels of income but gaps remain large

%

1990 2009 2011 2013

Poorest quintile, Quintile 2, Quintile 3, Quintile 4, Richest quintile

Note: "Gross enrolment" in Panel B is the ratio of students of all ages that attend tertiary education and students within the official age group. Thus, if there is late or early enrolment, or repetition, the total enrolment can exceed the population of the age group that officially corresponds to the level of education – leading to ratios greater than 100%.

Source: Panels A and C: OECD elaboration based on CASEN (1990, 2009, 2011 and 2013). Panel B: World Development Indicators.

StatLink http://dx.doi.org/10.1787/888933302289

Improving the financial terms of the existing income contingent loan system to make it more attractive would help. In some OECD countries (including Australia, New Zealand and the United Kingdom) income-contingent loan systems achieve a good balance between effective cost recovery on the government side and the risks to the borrower of being unable to repay student loans. Income-contingent loans are also more equitable, since graduates' payments are in direct proportion to their income. But this is not enough.

Resolving financial constraints will not alone solve the inequality challenge in tertiary education. Evidence shows that low high school quality and grades, as well as insufficient parental involvement, pose higher obstacles to attending university than financial constraints (Frenette, 2007). To increase access to quality tertiary education the key is to focus on the right implementations of the reforms to improve compulsory education. But Chile should also seek to reduce horizontal inequalities, which relate to the kind of institutions and programmes students attend that determine subsequent labour market opportunities. Some population groups are systematically tracked into categories of institutions and programmes that are less resourced or recognised in terms of labour market rewards. This explains why many students in Chile express *ex post* regret over excessive student loan debt relative to their earnings potential. A possible explanation is that some students base educational choices on limited or inaccurate information on the costs and benefits of studying different subjects. Low-income students would also benefit from more support in the transition from secondary to tertiary education. Better career guidance and improved information about likely job prospects can help youth make informed decisions about the field of study they might like to specialise in, and help them to choose the best educational institution for them to attend.

A skills strategy would help to address mismatch problems

Differences in skill mismatch across countries are a major driver of low productivity growth (Adalet McGowan and Andrews, 2015). Evidence shows that skill mismatch is relatively high in Chile (Randstad Workmonitor, 2012). Integrating more people in the labour markets requires education systems that are flexible and responsive to the needs of the labour market, and young people having access to high-quality career guidance and further education that can help them to match their skills to prospective jobs. Chile should develop work-based learning programmes across different levels and types of education to better integrate students into the labour market. For instance, making internships compulsory to validate some university qualifications, like in France, or integrating work-based training into the university curricula, like in many UK universities, can enhance graduates' employability.

But university is not the only route to pursue further education. One way to prepare students for the labour market is through vocational education and training (VET) systems that aim at providing the technical skills needed for the labour market. The Chilean VET system provides learning opportunities in remote regions and support for students at risk and plays a key role in up-skilling and integrating young people into the labour market. But the system size remains among the smallest in the OECD. The government could thus establish a formal consultation framework between employers, unions and the VET system, adopting quality standards and apprenticeships to support and expand workplace training as an integral part of vocational programmes. It could also provide pedagogical training to VET teachers before they start teaching and develop the capacity to analyse and use data on labour market needs to guide the design of policies and improve decision making.

Tax reform for a more inclusive Chile

Chile's tax revenues are comparatively low. At 20.2% of GDP, Chile's tax-to-GDP ratio was the second lowest in the OECD in 2013, where the average is 33.7% of GDP. The narrow tax base and heavy dependence on indirect taxes greatly constrains public revenues, and explains why the level of expenditure on public goods has been insufficient to reduce inequality. More social expenditure is financed privately in Chile than in most OECD countries. Before the tax reform, important tax exemptions mainly benefitted higher-income earners and left a large share of natural resource rents untaxed. Evidence shows that, in practice, evasion and avoidance by the top income earners has been a significant contributor to the low impact of income taxes (Fairfield and Jorratt, 2014). Moreover, personal income tax revenues – while they have increased in recent years – remain very low.

The government introduced a major tax reform in 2014 that entered partially into force the last quarter of 2014, though some provisions will be phased in over the 2015-17 period. The law contains various provisions including (see O'Reilly et al., 2015):

- Extensive changes to the corporate income tax.
- A reduction in the top personal income tax rate from 40 to 35%.
- Broadening of the base of VAT on real estate.
- Increases in health-related taxes.
- Increased taxation of carbon and other pollutants.
- Measures to strengthen tax administration, improve compliance, reduce Base Erosion and Profit Shifting (BEPS), and deter evasion and avoidance.

The tax measures aim to raise an extra 3% of GDP. More than half of the increased revenues are forecasted to come from increased income taxation (1½ per cent of GDP), mainly from corporate income. Increases in compliance are forecast to increase revenues by 0.52% of GDP, while expansions in the VAT base will account for 0.36% of GDP (Table 4).

Table 4. **Estimated increase in tax collection**

Measure	% of the projected revenue increase	% of GDP
Increase in collection due to plan to decrease tax evasion and avoidance	17.2	0.52
Other (taxing capital income of real estate, restrictions on deemed income system, etc.)	3.6	0.11
Effect of the repeal of several measures	3.3	0.10
Historical FUT incentive	1.7	0.05
New tax on contaminating motor vehicles	1.7	0.05
Effect tax change on alcoholic and non-alcoholic beverages	2.0	0.06
New tax on source emissions (CO_2, NO_x, PM)	2.3	0.07
Fiscal traceability of specific taxes and mining tax auditing	2.6	0.08
Taxing the sale of new properties and limiting the use of special VAT credit	11.9	0.36
Raising the stamp tax from 0.004 to 0.008	4.6	0.14
Change of tobacco tax	4.3	0.13
Corporate income tax	48.3	1.46
Decrease in collection due to saving incentives and others	-3.6	-0.11
Total	**100**	**3.02**

Source: Ministry of Finance of Chile.

The tax reform will help to reduce inequality by shifting the share of national income received by the top 1% of the population from 16.5% to 15.5% of GDP (World Bank, 2015). The reform increases tax progressivity, eliminates tax expenditures and fights tax evasion and avoidance. The envisaged gradualism of implementation is welcome, and it will remain important to monitor the effects on investment and savings, and be ready to adjust the reform if warranted.

The core of the tax reform will hike the statutory corporate tax rate by 7 percentage points, in Chile's semi-integrated tax system (O'Reilly et al., 2015). Although the overall tax burden is relatively low, the increase in the corporate tax rate will reposition Chile from one of the lowest corporate tax jurisdictions in the OECD to among the higher ones. Empirical evidence suggests that corporate taxes are the most damaging for economic growth, as they depress investment rates and reduce labour productivity (Arnold et al., 2011). However, Chile's semi-integrated system allows capital owners to use 65% of the corporate income tax as a credit for their personal income tax. While the reform's main goal is to raise additional revenue for social expenditure, further measures could be envisaged to improve the overall design of the tax system in the future. Notably, the personal income tax base is very narrow (OECD, 2013), in part due to the highly skewed income distribution. Taxes on real estate or immovable property remain underused, and would have lower efficiency costs. Helpfully, the reform already included a shift towards environmental taxes, in line with OECD recommendations, and such taxes that internalise negative externalities can be expanded in the future.

Improving the pension system is important to address inequality

In most OECD countries, pensions explain a large share of the overall redistributive impact of the tax and transfer system (OECD, 2012). In Chile, however, contributory pensions do not help to reduce inequality, as the Gini coefficient before and after pension contributions is very similar (Lustig, 2015). Although Chile's old-age pension system has reduced elderly poverty from around 23% in 2008 to 20% in 2011, thanks to a key reform in 2008 that enhanced the generosity of the pension system – by introducing an anti-poverty or "solidarity" pillar – the average pension remains only 15% of average earnings, although the standardised replacement rate is higher. Pensions are modest because they are primarily financed by mandatory contribution rates that remain low (10% of earnings – compared to 20% on average in the OECD), and low contribution patterns due to inconsistent work histories. Pensions become available for men at the age of 65 (same as the OECD average) and to women at the age of 60 (OECD average of 64).

The Chilean government set up an expert commission (*Comisión Asesora Presidencial sobre el Sistema de Pensiones*) to assess the pension system, identifying its strengths and limitations, and elaborate a set of remedies (Bravo et al., 2015). The commission examined a wide range of issues, but focused particularly on the large number of future pensioners who have low contribution densities. Overall, half of men have contribution densities lower than 47.5%, and half of women have densities of less than 12.8%. These low contribution histories are associated with work histories that include periods of self-employment, informal employment, unemployment or professional inactivity, and are particularly a problem for women and individuals in low income brackets.

The recommendations of the expert commission are highly consistent with OECD best practices. To make the pension system more sustainable and improve replacement rates, the required contribution rates should be gradually raised from 10% to 14%. In addition, to make the system more inclusive, reforms could focus on increasing the level of the solidarity pension (available to the bottom 60% of households), to improve replacement rates, notably for women and the poor. Changes in the system should increase the statutory retirement age, equalise the retirement age of men and women at 65 years, and periodically review the retirement age to be consistent with life expectancy. Finally, pension fund administration could be made more cost effective. These features are a key feature of sustainable pension systems. Programmes that interact with the pension system, and reduce the amount and incentives to contribute, such as social programmes *Fonasa* and Family Allowance, need to be revised. Reforms should also remove the modality of programmed retirement pension to avoid decreasing pensions over time, by encouraging annuitisation.

Labour reform should focus on protecting workers for a more inclusive labour market

High wage inequality in Chile is an important driver of overall inequality. Indeed, evidence shows that income inequality before taxes and transfers reflects mainly differences in labour market outcomes, as they account for around 75% of household income inequality across OECD countries, much more than the 25% accounted by self-employment and capital income combined (OECD, 2012). In part, this is because some of the countervailing forces and labour market institutions that favour redistribution in Chile, principally unions, collective bargaining mechanisms and statutory minimum wages, have a limited reach. As a result, union density and coverage are relatively low, and strongly concentrated in the public sector, affecting the wage distribution (OECD, 2011). Therefore, the proposed labour reform that would bring collective bargaining processes closer to those of other OECD countries makes sense (Chapter 1). Notably, clarifying the right to strike is a step forward to protect workers' rights, but it should be balanced.

The reform focuses almost exclusively on collective bargaining rules, and does not address the high degree of labour market duality that is a consequence of imbalanced protection of regular employment contracts as compared with temporary contracts. This divergence in protection creates duality in the labour market that feeds high job turnover and precariousness (Figure 13). Current legislation provides strong protection for employees with indefinite contracts, while providing little security to workers in non-standard contracts, increasing the level of income inequality (OECD, 2011). Temporary workers are worse off in many aspects of job quality. They tend to receive less training and, in addition, have more job strain and have less job security than workers in standard jobs. Earnings levels are also lower in terms of annual and hourly wages. Evidence shows that temporary workers in OECD countries face a significant wage penalty, even after controlling for observable individual, family and work characteristics (OECD, 2015a).

Legislation should focus on protecting workers rather than jobs. To rebalance job protection, Italy and Spain have introduced a single standard contract applying only to new employment contracts, with employment protection increasing with tenure. This new contract provides a basic level of protection for the first two years, after which the level of compensation for unfair dismissal increases. As evidence becomes available about the benefits, and possible costs of the single contract in Italy and Spain, Chile could usefully draw lessons.

Figure 13. **Workers on temporary contracts face very high rates of job turnover**

Annual job creation and destruction rates

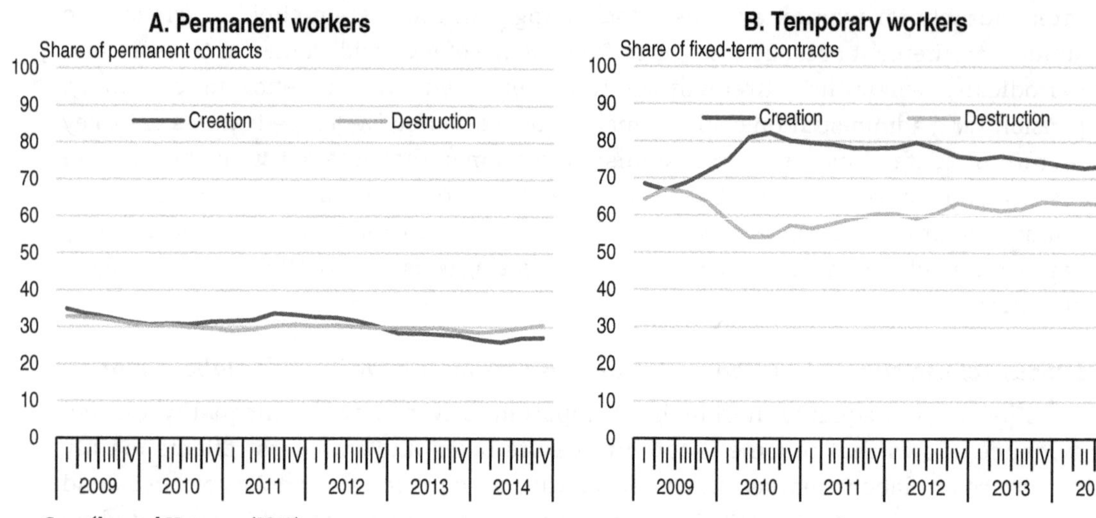

Source: González and Huneeus (2015).

StatLink http://dx.doi.org/10.1787/888933302298

Raising female participation is essential

Gender gaps contribute significantly to income inequality in Chile (OECD, 2012), even though many women have joined the labour market, as female participation increased from below 40% in the early 2000s to 55.7% in 2014. Gender gaps in employment and earnings persist: women are still less likely to being in paid work, to progress in their career and are more likely to earn less in their job (women earn 16% less than men). Considerable differences remain in the type and quality of jobs held by women and in their working hours, which can be partly attributed to social stereotypes about gender roles. Reducing the labour force participation gap between men and women by 50% has been estimated to raise annual growth in GDP per capita by 0.3 percentage points on average (OECD, 2012b). But it can also contribute to reduce income inequality, as evidence from OECD countries shows that having more women in paid (full-time) work results in lower household income inequality (Harkness, 2010; OECD, 2015).

Raising female participation is a top priority for the government. Its initial emphasis has been on rapidly expanding the availability of public childcare institutions through the"National Care Programme". To reinforce this effort, additional spending on active labour-market policies to boost participation is needed. Evidence shows that active labour market policies are potentially very important to bring women into employment as the average effects of these programmes are larger for women than for men (Bergemann and Van den Berg, 2008). This is because women's labour supply is more elastic than men's, and therefore participation in a programme that increases labour market opportunities, like a successful skill-enhancing training programme, may subsequently lead to job offers that are acceptable. Not surprisingly, Chile is one of OECD countries with the highest gender gap in labour force participation and with the lowest level of public spending devoted to active labour-market policies (Figure 14). The government has put in place a new programme, *MasCapaz* that will expand spending in labour-market programmes by 0.4% of GDP and contribute to increase women's labour participation and reduce the gender gap. The first-ever ministry on women is being created, which is in charge of promoting women rights.

Figure 14. **Gender gaps in labour force participation and spending on active labour market policies**

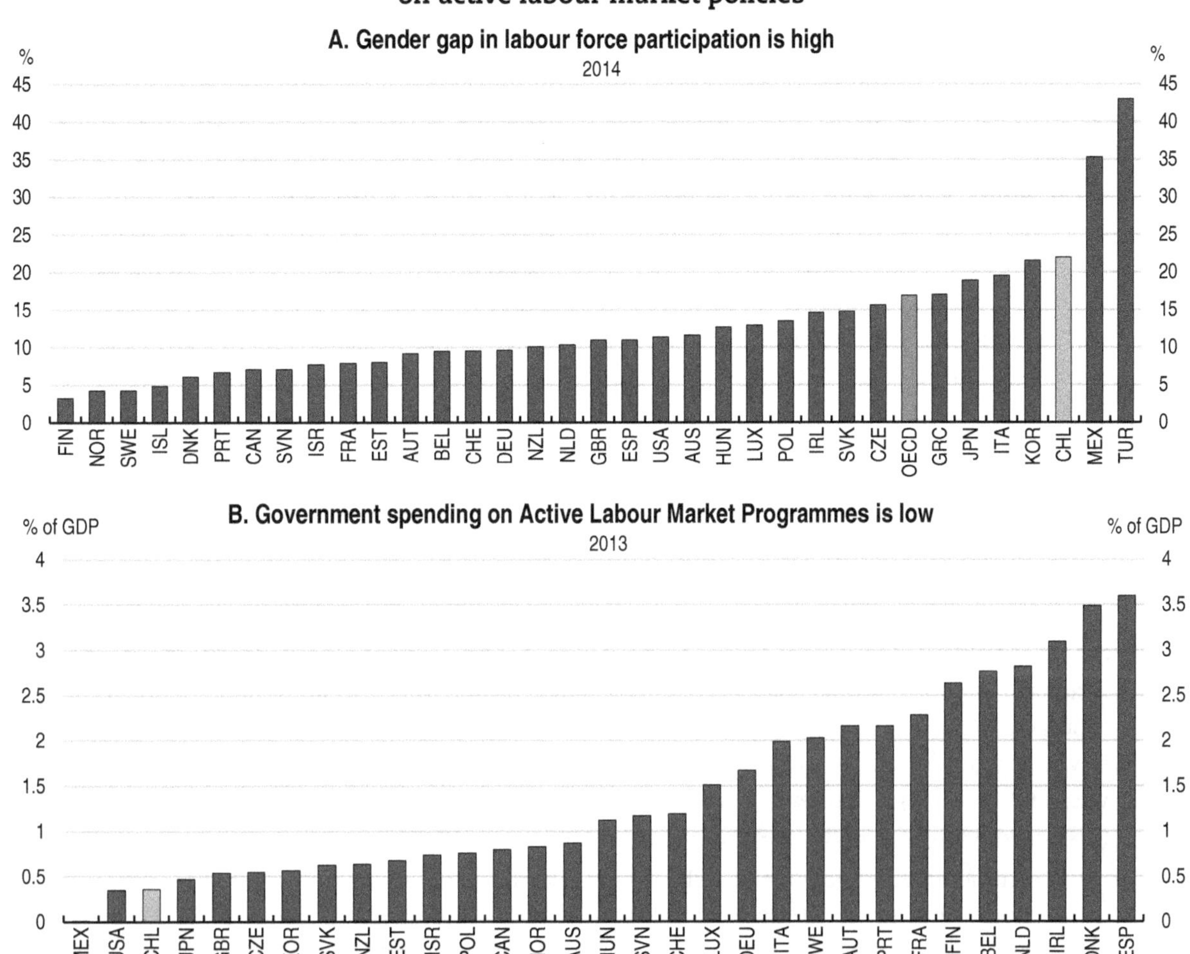

Note: The figure for Chile does not include the recent programme *MasCapaz*, which will increase spending on labour market policies by 0.4% of GDP.

Source: *OECD Employment and Labour Market Statistics.*

StatLink http://dx.doi.org/10.1787/888933302304

Boosting productivity and investment

Boosting productivity growth is perhaps Chile's foremost challenge to raise living standards. Unfortunately, Chile's productivity growth has trended at below zero for much of the past two decades (OECD, 2013a, 2015c), although outside of the capital-intensive mining sector, total factor productivity growth has been positive (Figure 15). Chile has improved its policy settings in recent years, but the intensity of competition in some sectors is weak and overall spending on R&D – particularly by the business sector – remains very low (Figure 16). Regulatory reforms and further administrative simplification will help open up pathways for entrepreneurship and investment, including through boosting infrastructure. Chile also needs to act on a number of fronts to improve the economy's innovation potential. Among the wide-ranging structural reforms that have been proposed by the administration, the Agenda for Productivity, Innovation and Growth seeks to address longstanding weaknesses in these areas.

Figure 15. **Total factor productivity with and without mining**

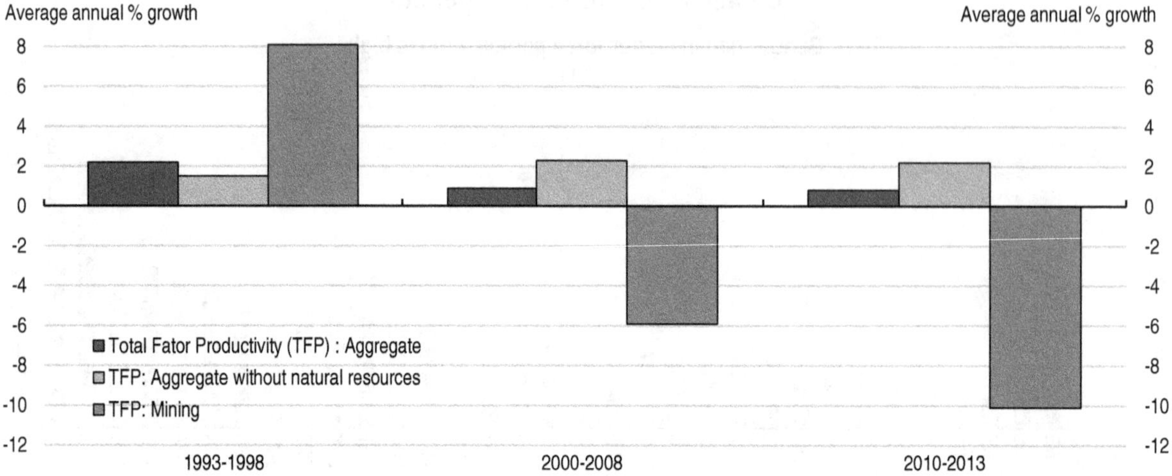

Source: UAI/CORFO (2014), *Boletín trimestral Evolución de la PTF en Chile*, No. 7.

StatLink http://dx.doi.org/10.1787/888933302315

An important component of the Agenda is institutional strengthening. Excessive fragmentation of the innovation system has been a longstanding problem that was discussed in previous *Economic Surveys of Chile* (OECD, 2013a) and earlier reviews of innovation policy (OECD, 2007). While the government has considered institutional reorganisation (Rivas et al., 2015), consensus for a new Ministry has not been achieved as of yet. At a minimum, the strengthening of the Inter-ministerial Committee on Innovation, with an explicit legal framework, and the National Council of Innovation for Development (CNID), which helps set longer-term strategy, seems warranted.

The Productivity Agenda also helps to address the fragmented institutional set-up for innovation by giving priority to a coherent set of targeted policies. It includes 47 different measures, focused around promoting the diversification of production, boosting sectors with high growth potential, the expansion of programmes and resources available for early-stage start-ups, boosting the competitiveness of businesses and generating a new impetus to exporting and attracting investments by reshaping the Foreign Investment Committee. The Agenda includes new funding of over USD 1.5 Billion, focusing on public-private co-operation. Over half of the measures have been implemented so far. Among the most notable of these endeavours is the creation of a Productivity Commission that will help to ensure that productivity is the focus of policymaking across the government.

As part of the Productivity Agenda, the administration announced the creation of a Productivity Commission in July 2015. Initially, the Commission has been set up by decree, and is a standing advisory body. This group of experts will carry out analyses and make recommendations relating to the design, implementation and evaluation of policies and reforms to directly stimulate productivity in Chile. The Commission may also prepare studies and regular reports, publish data and information and make proposals in areas they identify as priorities. This new body has considerable potential to strengthen the policymaking process, and help to identify the best way forward in a range of areas. Based on the pioneering experience of Australia, such bodies can help to address weaknesses in the policymaking process, by helping to develop consensus over contentious issues, based

Figure 16. **R&D expenditure and incentives**

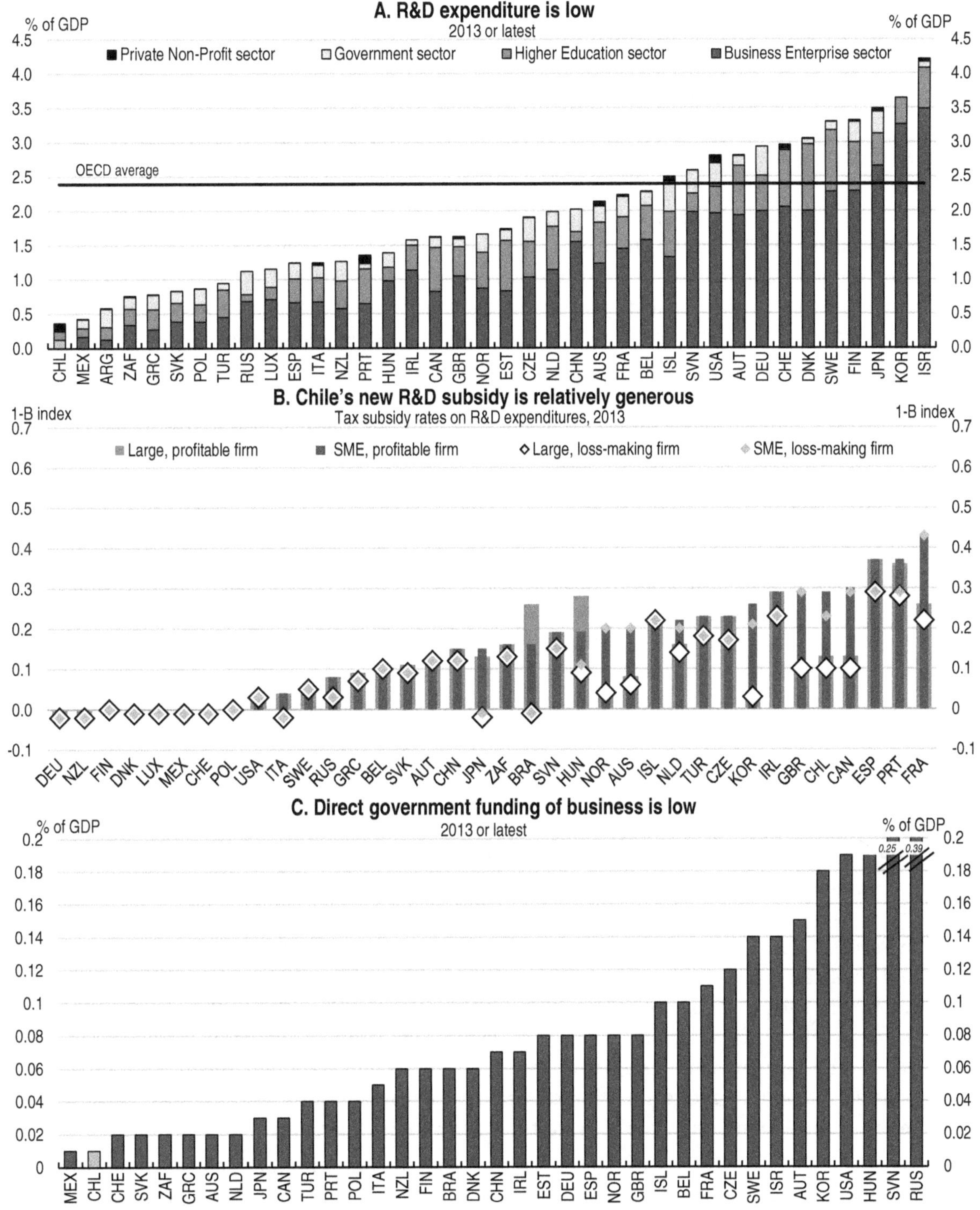

Note: Panel B: The tax subsidy rate is calculated as 1 minus the "B-index", a measure of the before-tax income needed to break even on USD 1 of R&D outlays. It is based on responses from national authorities and R&D statistical agencies to the OECD questionnaire on R&D tax incentives and also draws on other publicly available information. Benchmark tax data information, including statutory corporate income tax rates, is obtained from the OECD *Tax Database*, basic (non-targeted) corporate income tax rates.

Source: OECD (2015e), *OECD Science, Technology and Industry Scoreboard 2015: Innovation for growth and society.*

StatLink http://dx.doi.org/10.1787/888933302322

on their role as independent authorities. In this regard, it may be useful to give it a more formal and statutory role, including by introducing a requirement that government respond publicly and promptly to its recommendations (see Banks, 2015).

Strengthening the competition framework is crucial

Persistent lack of strength in Chile's productivity record can be partly traced to weaknesses in the competitive environment in product markets, where high market concentration is commonplace (Solimano, 2012). While Chile has made important improvements to its competition policy framework, some crucial features in the 2009 law are still missing (OECD, 2014a). The current system for reviewing mergers lacks clear merger control jurisdictional and substantive criteria, and relies instead on general antitrust procedures which were not designed for merger control purposes. Chile also lacks both an appropriate legal framework to carry out market studies and adequate resources to effectively perform them (OECD, 2015b). Market studies can lead to recommendations to private firms or public bodies aimed at removing any unnecessary obstacles to the working of markets, and if anticompetitive behaviours are detected they can lead to the opening of antitrust investigations.

The government is committed to reforming the competition law framework to ensure effective competition enforcement. A draft competition bill is currently in Congress, covering a new set of sanctions for cartels, a reformed system for merger control and market studies. The proposed reform is in line with OECD best practices and previous recommendations to Chile. The core of the reform increases the effectiveness of sanctions against illegal cartels: it promotes the introduction of criminal sanctions for executives and a higher ceiling for monetary fines. The OECD advocates a strong and effective system of sanctions to stamp out hard-core cartel behaviour, which is considered the most egregious violation of competition. The bill addresses these concerns by introducing a more effective and transparent merger control regime and granting the *Fiscalía Nacional Económica* formal powers to perform market studies.

Improving the regulatory environment will facilitate more dynamism

Another important barrier to productivity growth is the adverse impact of overly strict product market regulations. The OECD has recommended in previous *Economic Surveys* and in *Going for Growth* that administrative burdens on start-ups be further reduced, registration and notification requirements be eased and the bankruptcy regime be simplified. Major reforms in each of these areas have been undertaken, notably a law in 2013 that allows businesses to be started in only a day, and a bankruptcy law in 2014 that makes exit much easier. The new law is an important step in improving business dynamism. Better exit policies should improve reallocation of resources towards more productive uses, and by reducing uncertainty, stimulate both start-ups and venture financing.

Nevertheless, product market restrictiveness for Chile remains above the OECD member average, based on a standardised measure of stringency (Figure 17, Panel A). In some sectors, the state's involvement in business operations can be further aligned with best practice. For instance, regulatory procedures in some sectors are complex, which includes licensing requirements, and competition in some network sectors such as gas is hampered by still high entry barriers. Simulations based on countries with similar levels of

Figure 17. **Business regulation remains restrictive in multiple areas**

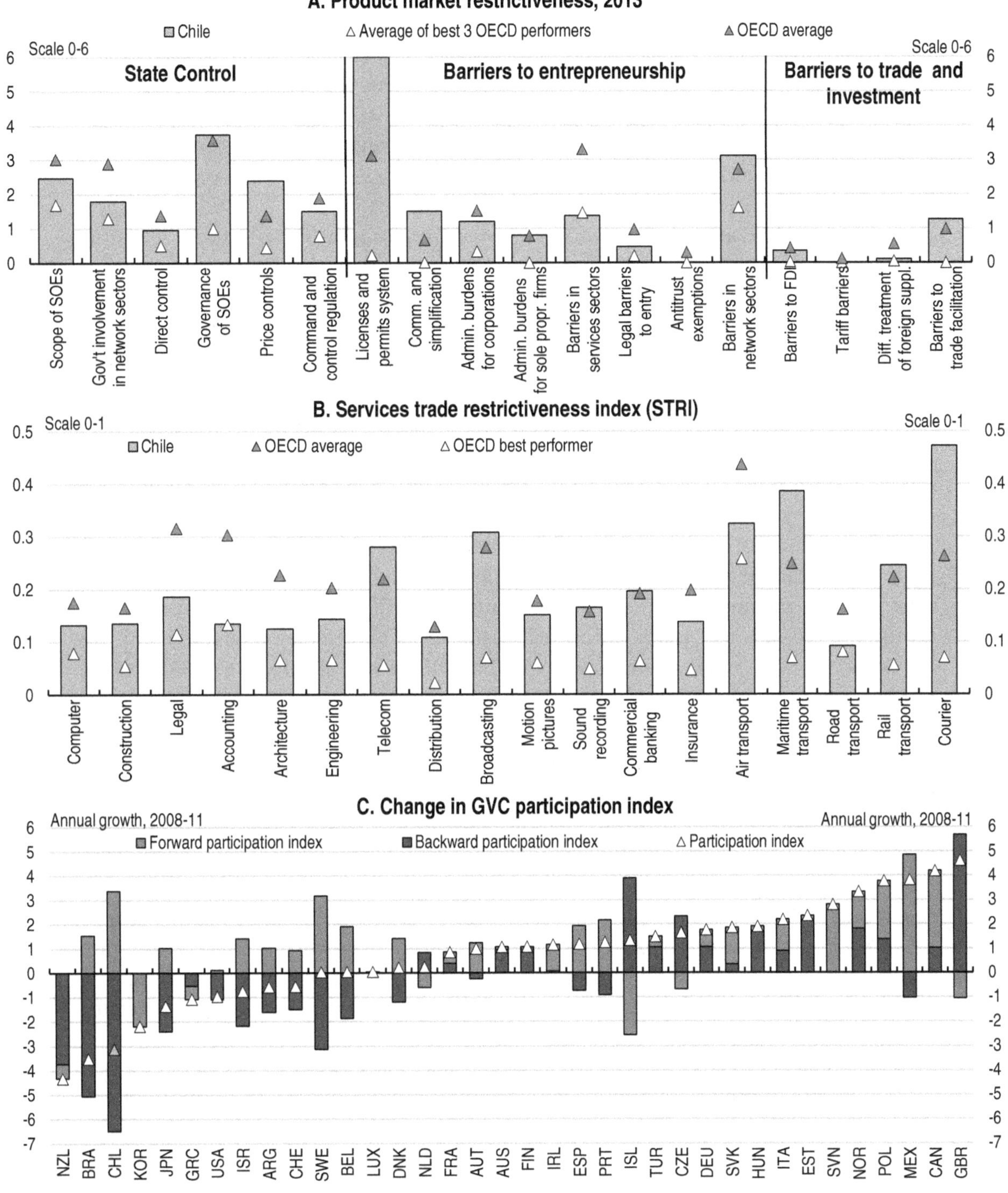

Note: The PMR indices take on a value of 0 to 6, from least to most stringent. More information is available at *www.oecd.org/eco/pmr*. The STRI indices take the value from 0 to 1, where 0 is completely open and 1 is completely closed. They are calculated on the basis of information in the *STRI Database* which reports regulation currently in force. For further information, see *www.oecd.org/tad/services-trade/services-trade-restrictiveness-index.htm*

Source: OECD, *Product Market Regulation Database, STRI Database, Trade in Value Added (TiVA) Database.*

StatLink http://dx.doi.org/10.1787/888933302333

restrictiveness (i.e. France and Mexico) suggest that aligning product market regulation with OECD best practice could boost GDP by ¼ to ½ per cent annually within five years (OECD, 2015c; IMF, 2015).

Further reforms of restrictions on trade in services (Figure 17, Panel B) could help to further improve Chile's integration into global value chains (OECD, 2015c, d, e). Open and coherent trade and investment policies can also be an important element of the pro-productivity reform agenda, and can facilitate local firms' participation in global value chains, which retrenched over the 2008 to 2011 period (Panel C). Exports and investment remain highly concentrated, and intermediary services such as maritime transport, telecommunications and courier services are some distance from best practice. Recognizing the need to facilitate further upgrading of value chains, as part of the Productivity Agenda, the Government passed a Foreign Investment Law in 2015, which introduced a new framework for investment promotion in Chile. This reform provides for a more pro-active investment strategy, and the government has moved towards establishing a reshaped investment promotion agency to ease the entry of foreign investors. It will be important that the approach continue to follow the OECD Policy Framework for Investment (OECD, 2015d).

The governance of state-owned enterprises (SOEs) could also be improved. In general, Chilean SOEs do well in matters relating to equal treatment of shareholders or stakeholders' engagement. However, there is a need to continue strengthening the governance of SOEs, including as part of Chile's commitments to OECD instruments in this area. For instance, appointments to the boards of SOEs should be merit-based and politicisation avoided; the boards should consist primarily of independent directors, ideally with private-sector experience skills. This specifically remains an issue with two key SOEs, the state mining company (ENAMI) and the state oil company (ENAP), whose corporate governance body have not yet been reformed.

Chile's national regulations provide the general framework for administrative procedures and an efficient state administration, but the lack of a comprehensive regulatory reform programme has reduced the possibilities to achieve even better economic outcomes (OECD, 2015f). Strong regulatory governance is needed to move forward and, according to OECD best practice, this will normally require a regulatory oversight body to give guidance to policymakers about regulatory issues that need to be fixed. Such a body would make systematic use of evidence-based regulatory impact assessments (RIA) to promote effective regulation to improve the effectiveness and efficiency of new and existing regulation. While Congress carries out *ex post* reviews of laws, fewer efforts have been made to introduce *ex ante* impact assessments (e.g. *Estatuto PyME*), and these have had limited success. Most importantly, there is no legal requirement for the benefits of new regulations to outweigh their costs, nor for the regulation to be underpinned by an explanation for its rationale. One successful comprehensive regulatory reform approach that has been used in the Netherlands is to review existing regulations with an objective of reducing redundant regulatory burdens in a targeted way, at the same time improving the overall quality of public policy objectives. A distinctive feature of the Dutch regulatory reform architecture are quantitative targets such as the net 25% reduction target for regulatory burdens imposed on businesses and aimed at improving regulatory efficiency inside government, complemented by a dashboard of qualitative indicators. Introducing "zero licensing procedures", as was done in Portugal, could also help. This is a simplified regime that allows for starting or modifying certain economic activities with a simple declaration through a single electronic point of contact.

Successful innovation promotion programmes could develop new fields

Competition and innovation are closely interlinked, and Chile's low total factor productivity growth is also linked to weaknesses in its innovation system. In addition to raising productivity growth, innovation is critical for diversifying the economy away from mining. Chile has improved its policy settings in recent years, but R&D and innovation spending – particularly by the business sector – remain very low, despite an eased and expanded R&D subsidy scheme (Figure 16, Panel B) that has been gaining traction among companies. Nevertheless, Chile remains the lowest overall R&D performer in the OECD, at under ½ per cent of GDP (OECD, 2015e).

Previous *Economic Surveys* have recommended that Chile could strengthen its innovation programmes by thoroughly evaluating them (OECD, 2013). These programmes are often well-designed, but they struggle to address a long-standing divide between businesses and universities in the innovation system, although National Innovation Policy (2014-18) includes programmes that specifically target this problem. Often, programme scale and take-up have not been large enough to make a substantial impact, with only 1% of companies in the formal sector taking part. The government is currently carrying out pilot evaluations of 1 in 10 of the programmes, and plans to begin a comprehensive implementation in 2016.

More broadly, a new effort is being devoted to Strategic Programmes (*Programas Estratégicos*), which foster public-private co-ordination in potentially high growth sectors, and could help to foster the emergence of clusters. While the OECD has previously urged caution on certain cluster-based approaches (OECD, 2013), greater concentration of public support (including provision of infrastructure) can be appropriate if it is done in a way that emphasises industry-science co-operation and seeks to promote on-going dialogue among government, private firms and other stakeholders (see Dougherty, 2015; Wagner, 2015). OECD reviews suggest that addressing co-ordination problems and focusing on creating networks, such as a framework for dialogue among government, private firms and other stakeholders, is the most effective approach (Warwick, 2013). This is the approach that the new Programme follows, which will require follow-through to be successful, conditional on it being positively evaluated. Chile's copper deposits for mining, waters for fish farming, soils for wine making, clear skies for astronomy and high radiation for solar power are important assets for developing science and cross-links that can help generate a local innovation eco-system and strengthen technological development. Efforts should seek to build on comparative advantage, with caution exercised to avoid creating opportunities for rent-seeking behaviour, through continued monitoring and regular evaluations of different support programmes as well as a strong involvement of the private sector (OECD, 2015h).

Environmental challenges are being addressed

Chile adopted a Green Growth Strategy in 2013, which is now being updated and broadened to reflect the new administration's concerns on ecosystems, health and gender. The country continues to face high levels of air pollution, particularly in areas with high population density and surrounding mining areas, with the poor most heavily exposed (OECD, 2015g). Heavy reliance on (imported) fossil fuels has made control of emissions difficult (Figure 18). However, the renewable target of 20% by 2020 should be met, and the new administration's agenda on energy aims to improve incentives further, to achieve its latest commitment to reduce CO_2 emissions per unit of GDP by 30% relative to 2007 levels.

Figure 18. **CO_2 intensity of electricity**

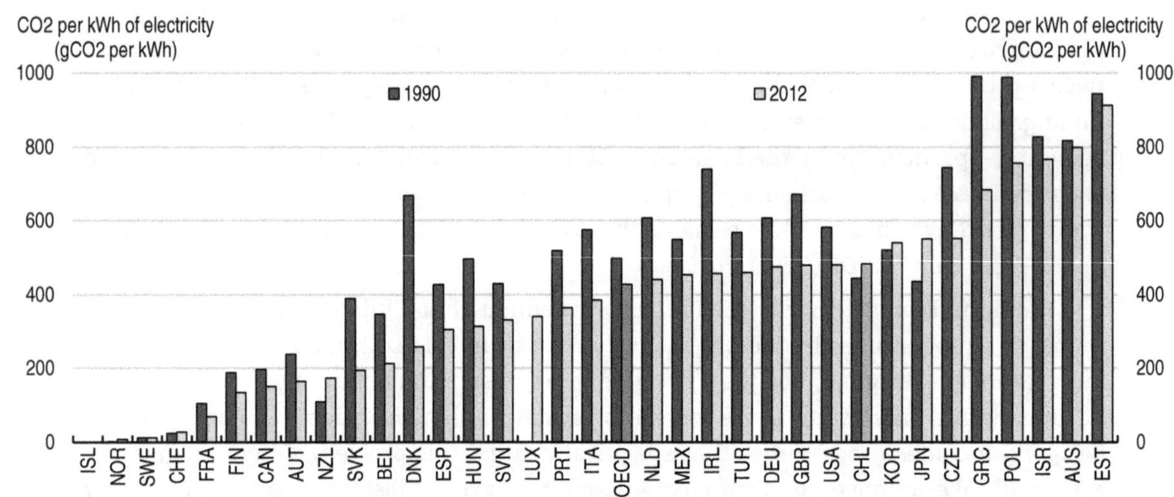

Note: This data should be used with caution due to data quality problems relating to electricity efficiencies for some countries.
Source: International Energy Agency, CO_2 *Emissions from Fuel Combustion Statistics.*

StatLink http://dx.doi.org/10.1787/888933302341

Important progress has occurred in the area of green taxes, although the level of these taxes is below the OECD average. Chile introduced a tax on new vehicles to raise revenues as well as to orient consumers towards less polluting vehicles. The tax entered into force in December 2014. It is paid only once, before the vehicle is registered, based on the vehicle's emissions of nitrogen oxides (NO_x) and its selling price. Nevertheless, due to exemptions, implied tax rates on transport fuels are among the lowest in the OECD, and Chile could advance on removing exemptions on fuels to align with the social costs of environmental damages. Such taxes on fuels have the additional advantage of being generally progressive with respect to incomes (Flues and Thomas, 2015).

Chile also introduced an innovative tax on emissions from stationary sources of pollution, from 2017, which will significantly broaden the energy tax base and might set an example for other countries. The tax includes two components: a carbon tax at a rate of USD 5 per ton of CO_2 and a tax on local pollutants (SO_2, NO_x, PM) which takes into account the social cost of pollution, the dispersion of pollutants and the size of the population exposed. However, the proposed carbon tax still falls well short of the actual social costs of carbon (OECD, 2015g) and should be raised to cover these social costs, as well as to help spur long-term investment in low-carbon technologies.

Bibliography

Adalet McGowan, M. and D. Andrews (2015), "Labour Market Mismatch and Labour Productivity: Evidence from PIAAC Data", *OECD Economics Department Working Papers*, No. 1209.

Ahmed, S., M. Appendino and M. Ruta (2015), "Depreciations without Exports? Global Value Chains and the Exchange Rate Elasticity of Exports", *World Bank Policy Research Working Paper*, No. 7390.

Albagi, E. et al. (2015), "Crecimiento Tendencial de Mediano Plazo en Chile", *Minutas Citadas en IPoM*, September.

Arnold, J., B. Brys, C. Heady, A. Johansson, C. Schwellnus and L. Vartia (2011), "Tax Policy for Economic Recovery and Growth", *The Economic Journal*, Vol. 121, Issue 550, pp. F59-F80.

Banks, G. (2015), "Institutions to Promote Pro-Productivity Policies: Logic and Lessons", *OECD Productivity Papers*, forthcoming.

Bravo, D. et al. (2015), *Presidential Advisory Commission on the Chilean Pension System*, Santiago, *www.comision-pensiones.cl*.

Castelletti, B. (2013), "How redistributive is fiscal policy in Latin America? The cases of Chile and Mexico", *OECD Development Centre Working Papers*, No. 318.

Ceballos, L. and D. Romero (2014), "Risk Matters: The Impact of Nominal Uncertainty in Chile", *Central Bank of Chile Working Papers*, No. 741.

Central Bank of Chile (2015a), *Financial Stability Report*, Santiago, June.

Central Bank of Chile (2015b), *Monetary Policy Report*, Santiago, September.

Dougherty, S. (2015), "Boosting Growth and Reducing Informality in Mexico", *OECD Economics Department Working Papers*, No. 1188, March.

Engel, E. et al. (2015), *Consejo Asesor Presidencial Contra los Conflictos de Interés, el Tráfico de Influencias y la Corrupción* (Presidential Advisory Council Against Conflicts of Interest, Influence Peddling and Corruption), Santiago, April, *www.consejoanticorrupcion.cl/informe*.

Fairfield, T. and M. Jorratt De Luis (2015), "Top Income Shares, Business Profits, and Effective Tax Rates in Contemporary Chile", *Review of Income and Wealth*, forthcoming.

Flues, F. and A. Thomas (2015), "The distributional effects of energy taxes", *OECD Taxation Working Papers*, No. 23, OECD, Paris.

González, S. and C. Huneeus (2015), "Job Creation and Destruction in Chile: 2009-14", Chilean Ministry of Labour and Social Affairs, Santiago Mimeo.

IMF (2015), *Chile: 2015 Article IV Consultation*, International Monetary Fund, Washington, DC.

Johansson, A., Y. Guillemette, F. Murtin, D. Turner, G. Nicoletti, C. de la Maisonneuve, P. Bagnoli, G. Bousquet and F. Spinelli (2012), "Long-run growth scenarios", *OECD Economics Department Working Papers*, No. 1000.

Kowalski, P. et al. (2015), "Participation of Developing Countries in Global Value Chains: Implications for Trade and Trade-Related Policies", *OECD Trade Policy Papers*, No. 179, OECD, Paris.

Lustig, N. (2015), "Inequality and Fiscal Redistribution in Middle Income Countries: Brazil, Chile, Colombia, Indonesia, Mexico, Peru and South Africa", *Center for Global Development Working Papers*, No. 410, August.

OECD (2010, 2012a, 2013a), *OECD Economic Surveys: Chile*, OECD Publishing, Paris.

OECD (2012b, 2013b), *OECD Employment Outlook*, OECD Publishing, Paris.

OECD (2014a), *Assessment of Merger Review in Chile*, OECD, Paris.

OECD (2014b), *OECD Rural Policy Reviews: Chile 2014*, OECD Publishing, Paris.

OECD (2014c), *Chile's Supreme Audit Institution: Enhancing Strategic Agility and Public Trust*, OECD Publishing, Paris.

OECD (2015a), *Economic Policy Reforms 2015: Going for Growth*, OECD Publishing, Paris.

OECD (2015b), *Competition and Market Studies in Latin America*, OECD, Paris.

OECD (2015c), *Chile: Policy Priorities for Stronger and more Equitable Growth*, OECD, Paris.

OECD (2015d), *Policy Framework for Investment, 2015 Edition*, OECD Publishing, Paris.

OECD (2015e), *OECD Science, Technology and Industry Scoreboard 2015: Innovation for growth and society*, OECD Publishing, Paris.

OECD (2015f), *A Diagnostic of Chile's Engagement in Global Value Chains*, OECD, Paris, forthcoming.

OECD (2015g), *Regulatory Reform Review of Chile*, OECD, Paris, forthcoming.

OECD (2015h), *Environmental Policy Review of Chile*, OECD, Paris, forthcoming.

OECD (2015i), *Universal Basic Skills: What Countries Stand to Gain*, OECD Publishing, Paris.

O'Reilly, P., S. Perret, B. Brys and M. Harding (2015), "Assessment of the 2014 Tax Reform in Chile", *Technical Background Paper*, OECD Centre for Tax Policy.

Rivas, G. et al. (2015), *Comisión Presidencial Ciencia Para el Desarrollo de Chile* (Presidential Commission for the Development of Science in Chile), National Innovation Council for Development (CNID), Santiago.

Rojas-Suarez, L. (2015). "Basel III in Chile: Advantages, Disadvantages and Challenges for Implementing the New Bank Capital Standard", *Center for Global Development CGD Policy Paper*, No. 061.

Solimano, A. (2012), *Chile and the Neoliberal Trap: The Post-Pinochet Era*, Cambridge University Press, Santiago.

Wagner, R. (2015), "How Could Chile Target Productivity Policies?", CNID, *Manuscript*, *www.cnid.cl*.

Warwick, K. (2013), "Beyond Industrial Policy: Emerging Issues and New Trends", *OECD Science, Technology and Industry Working Papers*, No. 2013/2.

ANNEX

Progress in structural reform

The objective of this annex is to review action taken since the previous Survey *(October 2013) on the main recommendations from previous* Surveys, *which are not reviewed and assessed in the current* Survey.

Past OECD recommendations	Actions taken since the 2013 *Survey*
A. Sustaining rapid growth	
Maintain the sound macroeconomic policy framework. If short-term downside risks materialise, ease monetary policy and, as foreseen in the fiscal rule, allow automatic stabilisers to work.	The credibility of the Central Bank has allowed it to implement an expansionary monetary policy. The policy rate has decreased 200 basis points from 5% in October 2013 to 3% today, supporting investment and consumption. The inflation-targeting framework has allowed the exchange rate to depreciate around 10% in real terms since beginning of 2013, contributing to absorb the adverse external shocks. Even with the weaker exchange rate putting upward pressure on prices – increasing inflation above the Central Bank's target range – rate cuts have been possible as inflation expectations have remained well-anchored at 3%. Fiscal policy in 2015 has included a 9.8% increase in public expenditures, mainly directed towards public investment, which will rise by 27.5%. A strong financial and fiscal position allowed the government to deploy its automatic stabilisers and to commit to an effective countercyclical fiscal policy.
In view of Chile's situation as a small open economy subject to substantial external shocks, medium-term budget targets should be consistent with maintaining a strong government net financial position.	To maintain the country's solid fiscal position and its responsible approach towards public finance, the government is committed to a steady process of fiscal consolidation beginning from 2016, and to a structural balance balanced budget position in the medium term.
As the Chilean economy advances, equity and well-being more broadly would benefit from the further development of high quality education and efficient, well-evaluated social protection programmes. These should be funded by fighting tax evasion and, if needed, through non-distortionary tax measures.	In 2014, the government passed an ambitious tax reform to raise revenues (by around 3% of GDP) to fund higher social spending and investment in education and health care, and improve the level of fairness in the tax code to contribute to reduce inequality. Other measures of the tax reform included modification of several aspects of the corporate tax system to mitigate distortions and opportunities for tax avoidance, and established a General Anti-Avoidance Rule which forbids aggressive tax avoidance.
Establish a legal framework for consolidated supervision of financial conglomerates and give legal status to the Financial Stability Council.	In 2014, a law granting legal status to the Financial Stability Council was enacted, which also introduced amendments to the laws governing the Financial Superintendencies (Banks, Securities and Insurance, and Pensions). Regarding oversight and supervision of financial conglomerates, the new legislation includes substantial improvements, including enabling financial supervisors to request and share information regarding the financial situation of any other entity belonging to the conglomerate. In addition, the law includes new solvency requirements for controlling partners of banks and insurance companies. The Chilean government is also currently receiving technical assistance from the International Monetary Fund to further improve conglomerate supervision.
Enhance independence of the banking supervisory authority, and review the legal framework for bank resolution.	In May 2015, the government started working on a new framework for banking supervision that incorporates international standards and best practices regarding capital requirements and composition; creates a modern and effective resolution procedure, and strengthens the corporate governance of the regulator.
Strengthen the institutional setup of the statistical system with better funding and staffing of the National Statistical Institute and ensure that core methodologies follow OECD best practices.	A bill was submitted to Congress in October 2015 to strengthen the statistical system and provide additional funding to the National Statistical Institute. New methods are being introduced, including a time use survey in 2015-16 based on OECD recommendations.
Further enhance the transparency and accountability of the fiscal framework by strengthening the independence of the newly constituted Fiscal Advisory Council.	The Government is working together with the Fiscal Advisory Council, the IMF, experts from universities, think tanks, and other research-based organisations, in the definition of key aspects of a new Fiscal Responsibility Law to further improve institutions concerned with fiscal policy.

Past OECD recommendations	Actions taken since the 2013 *Survey*
B. Strengthening green growth	
Formulate and adopt a fully-fledged green growth strategy, including policies to achieve recently-introduced emission and renewable energy targets. Fully reflect the social costs of externalities with pricing mechanisms, such as raising excise taxes and removing tax exemptions on fuels.	Chile adopted a Green Growth Strategy in 2013, and it is now being updated to the new challenges of the country. The new green growth strategy will be ready in the first quarter of 2016. Chile adopted Green Taxes on stationary sources and mobile sources in the tax reform on 2014; a tax on CO_2 emissions and local contaminants from stationary sources with boilers and turbines, and a tax on the first sale of new cars based on expected NO_x emissions over their lifetime. The new taxes explicitly consider the social costs of externalities. They will be fully implemented in 2017 (the tax on cars will be introduced gradually from 2015 to 2017).
Develop effective mechanisms to optimise water use in areas where water rights have been over-allocated, such as through the buying-back or forfeiture of unused water rights.	One of the main problems with water use efficiency is the over-allocation of water rights. This issue is being partially addressed within the discussions of the Water Code Reform, which would restrict certain rights depending on the aquifer conditions.
Enforce the recently-adopted obligations for owners of mining licenses to clean up polluted sites and reduce emissions. Intensify work with the mining industry to rehabilitate abandoned mining sites.	Many actions have been taken in order to implement the law that deals with mine site closure, which entered into force in November 2012. In November 2014, Sernageomin (National Service of Geology and Mining) ended the transitional system and in March 2015 the Ministry of Mining carried out an amendment to the regulation. To date, 140 mine site closure plans from mine sites of more than 10 thousand tons per month have been submitted, out of which some are still subjected to the evaluation process carried out by Sernageomin. Regarding abandoned mining sites, the Ministry of Mining and Sernageomin have carried out several actions, including identification and a cadastre of liabilities; research on risk evaluation methodologies; and economic evaluations to compare between different alternatives, among others.
Carry out a review of natural resource rents and ensure that they are taxed sufficiently to ensure sustainable development.	No actions taken.

Main recent OECD recommendations	Actions taken since the 2013 *Survey*
C. Making labour markets more inclusive	
Increase female workforce participation by expanding high-quality childcare, promoting flexible working hours and providing non-transferable parental leave entitlements to fathers. To increase childcare take-up, continue to publicise the availability of childcare options.	The current government is building more than 3 000 child care centres during the period 2014-18, and expanding spaces in existing establishments.
Boost youth employment by expanding the reduced minimum wage for youth under 18 to those under 25 years old and implementing the reformed apprenticeship contracts. In parallel with extending unemployment benefits, lower the relatively high severance pay for regular workers.	The government appointed a wage commission that will deliver a proposal for the minimum wage in the second half of 2015. Also, the government will continue providing the *Subsidio al Empleo Joven* and the *Subsidio Previsional a los Trabajadores Jóvenes* in order to increase levels of youth employment in the formal sector.
Strengthen the public training framework through quality standards and performance assessments for training providers, and by better targeting low-skilled workers. Improve job search assistance by strengthening local employment offices.	The government launched last year the programme *+Capaz* that will train 300 000 women and 150 000 youth over 2014-18. The focus will be low skilled workers and those with weak labour market attachment.
Carry out pilot studies using private sector providers for personalised job counselling of harder-to-place jobseekers.	No actions taken.
Strengthen vocational education by updating curricula, further developing work placement and by deepening the on-going standardised qualification framework to boost mobility.	No actions taken.
Eliminate the requirement for firms to finance childcare once they employ 20 women or more.	The current government is working on a reform proposal on this issue.
Extend unemployment benefits further, as planned, and exploit this by monitoring job search efforts and improving job search assistance.	A reform was passed in April 2015 extending unemployment benefits. Current changes in the monitoring of job search efforts and job search assistance will be implemented through the *Bolsa Nacional de Empleo* and the OMIL in the second half of 2015.

Main recent OECD recommendations	Actions taken since the 2013 *Survey*
D. Boosting entrepreneurship and innovation	
Co-ordination among the various innovation policymaking agencies could be improved by establishing the Ministry of Innovation recently proposed.	In early 2015 a Presidential Commission was convened to propose institutional changes in the area of science, technology and innovation. The report was presented in July 2015. It includes recommendations for two alternative models that will help to strengthen co-ordination among different agencies. Additionally, a ministerial-level committee for innovation, including ministers of Economy, Education, and Finance among others, meets regularly to co-ordinate actions in the area on innovation.
Further facilitate industry and research linkages, and promote public-private co-ordination to exploit natural endowments, such as for copper mining, helping to complement comparative advantages.	In 2014 and 2015 new programmes aimed at increasing the linkage between universities and companies were launched: an innovation voucher and a R&D firm-university contract instrument. The programme that co-funds firms hiring of PhDs and masters has recently been expanded. At the institutional level, a Technology Transfer Inter-ministerial committee was created. The objective is to establish a common policy across governmental agencies in order to incorporate tech transfer variables in University Financing rules as part of the Educational Reform. In 2015, the Ministry of Economy and CORFO launched a Strategic Programme on Intelligent Specialization. These are public-private co-ordination initiatives in the areas of Mining, Aquaculture, Solar Energy, Logistics, Tourism, "Intelligent Industries" (ICT), Healthy Foods and Sustainable Construction. Each programme will identify sector-specific gaps and will propose technological roadmaps to increase productivity and competitiveness.
Regularly review innovation programmes, close down or adjust inefficient ones, and expand those that are proven to work.	The Ministry of Economy is implementing, at a pilot scale, an information platform of the National Innovation Systems, which aims to collect information on 15 of the 130 public aid instruments on Science, Technology, Innovation and Entrepreneurship. The pilot will cover 10 instruments at CORFO and 5 instruments at CONICYT. The main goal of the platform is to provide information and guidelines to evaluate programmes and instruments. Based on the results of the pilot, a full roll-out of the platform including 130 instruments will take place in 2016.
Over time, make the R&D tax credit refundable for smaller firms, so that young innovative start-ups can more easily benefit, and consider adding an element to the scheme that enhances rebates for incremental investments.	In 2016 the impact and results of the R&D tax credit law will be reviewed.
Expand advanced degree financial support on technological fields, especially in the Becas Chile programme.	No action taken. The regular calls for post degree scholarships "Becas Chile" are still neutral in their allocation. Nevertheless, the regulation of these calls does allow for targeting allocations in priority areas, which can be defined according to technological requirements.
Further boost access of entrepreneurs to global networks and venture capital, including by simplifying requirements for foreign venture capital funds to operate locally.	Support for entrepreneurs has been significantly increased over time; in 2015 the budget for entrepreneurship programmes was increased by 47%. Also, in 2015 a new instrument for early stage venture capital was launched. This new instrument is a combination of subsidies for operation and investment in the form of debt (in a 3:1 leverage). This new instrument will create a strong incentive to both local and foreign venture capital funds.

Thematic chapters

Chapter 1

Bringing all Chileans on board

The Chilean economy has had an extraordinary performance over the last decades with strong growth and declining poverty rates. However, the economy is now slowing at a time when inequality remains very high, making future social progress challenging. This chapter discusses how to achieve greater social inclusiveness against the background of weaker medium-term growth. First, it argues that Chile needs to increase income redistribution through its tax and transfer system towards levels prevailing in other OECD countries. Although existing social transfers are effective in combatting poverty, their size remains small and many households at the bottom of the ladder are not reached by them. Second, the chapter argues that labour earnings should be less disparate, as they explain around 70% of income inequality. This should be done by updating labour legislation, but also by empowering low-skill workers and enabling them to increase their productivity, through the acquisition of adequate skills. Finally, focus should be placed on closing wide gender gaps.

Chile has made tremendous progress over past decades improving the quality of life of its citizens. Since the 1990s, economic growth and poverty reduction achieved by Chile have been among the most impressive in the OECD. However, robust growth has not delivered inclusive prosperity as limited progress has been made to reduce overall income inequality (Figure 1.1), leaving Chile as one of the most unequal countries in the OECD. Addressing this challenge would contribute to sustainable long-run growth by raising social capital and public trust, and by reducing distributional conflict and crime, leading to higher factor accumulation and productivity improvements.

Figure 1.1. **Despite strong progress reducing poverty, high levels of inequality remain**

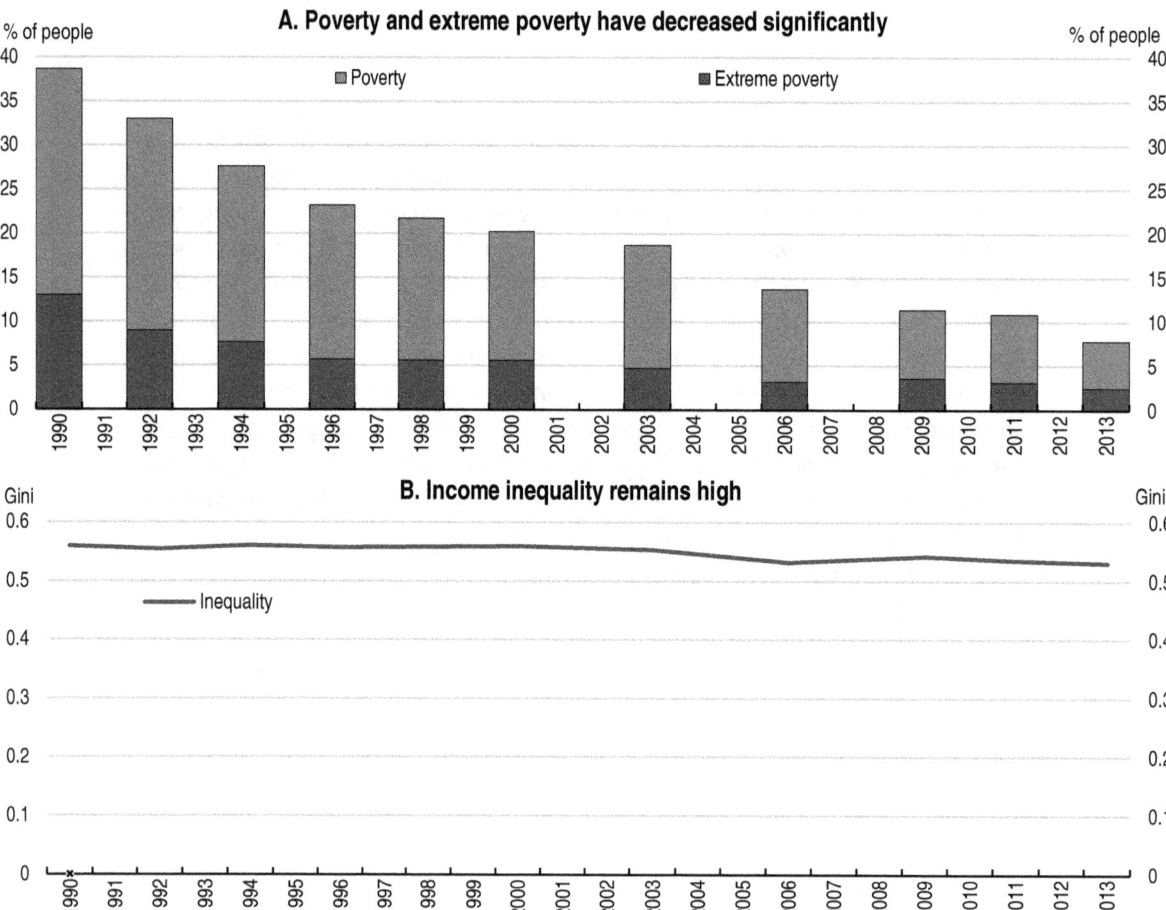

Note: The poverty line for a family of four is a family income below CLP 361 311 per month, and the extreme poverty line is a family income below CLP 240 874 per month, both for the year 2013.

Source: Ministerio de Desarrollo Social.

StatLink http://dx.doi.org/10.1787/888933302350

In 2014, the government adopted an ambitious and welcome policy agenda to reduce inequality. This includes a tax reform to raise more revenue and expand social programmes; an education reform to build more inclusive schools and reduce skill gaps across socio-economic groups; and a labour reform to expand the coverage and scope of collective bargaining. This chapter discusses some of these reforms (education is discussed in Chapter 2). After presenting key stylised facts, the chapter argues that reducing income inequality will contribute to social mobility and boost productivity growth. Then it discusses policies that are needed to promote income distribution. It suggests that bringing all Chileans on board requires focusing on: expanding and improving the efficiency of the tax-and-transfer systems for effective redistribution; tackling inequalities in the labour market to promote employment and good-quality jobs; and expanding women participation in the labour force to close gender gaps.

How inclusive is Chile?

Chile has experienced a remarkable decline in absolute poverty since the return to democracy in the 1990s. The share of people living below the national poverty line has fallen dramatically (see Figure 1.1). Strong economic growth, which increased labour income for all income deciles, social policies and a significant increase in educational attainment, explain in a large part the decrease in poverty rates. The development of a sophisticated system of transfers and subsidies – around 40% of the population receives cash transfers and subsidies provided by the state – has been relatively successful at lifting people out of poverty (Sunkel and Infante, 2009; Rau, 2011). However, the decline in inequality has been much more modest.

Chile continues to be one of the most unequal OECD countries (Figure 1.2). High inequality is mostly explained by the concentration of income at the top of the ladder: when the richest 10% of the population are excluded, the GINI index drops by 0.16 points, compared to a reduction of 0.06 points in the average OECD country. Households at the top of the income distribution get a large share of national income: the top 10% earns 26.5 times the average income of the bottom 10%, compared to an OECD average of 9.6 times. Similarly, wealth is concentrated at the top: while the bottom 40% holds only 1.65% of total income, the top 1% holds 21% (Lopez et al., 2013).

Another feature of Chile's inequality is the strong correlation between social class and the degree of indigenous ancestry. Evidence shows that 73-91% of the upper class has Caucasian genes, while 68-70% have this characteristic and only 40-45% of the lowest class (Diaz Vidal, 2014). Therefore, the major indigenous populations in Chile are overrepresented in the lowest deciles of the income distribution. And although in the past they used to be a rural population, today half of the indigenous population reside in Santiago (Diaz Vidal, 2014).

Reducing income inequality can help increase growth and promote social mobility

High inequality raises major economic concerns. It reduces trust (Uslaner and Brown, 2005), which is an important driver of long-term growth (Horváth, 2012); it also increases the probability of rent-seeking and political and economic "capture" by the economic elite (OECD, 2015a). Furthermore, inequality reduces the capacity of the poorer segments of the population to invest in their skills and education (OECD, 2015b). For instance, OECD estimates show that an increase in inequality of around 6 Gini points lowers the probability of poorer people

Figure 1.2. **Income inequality is especially high at the top of the distribution**

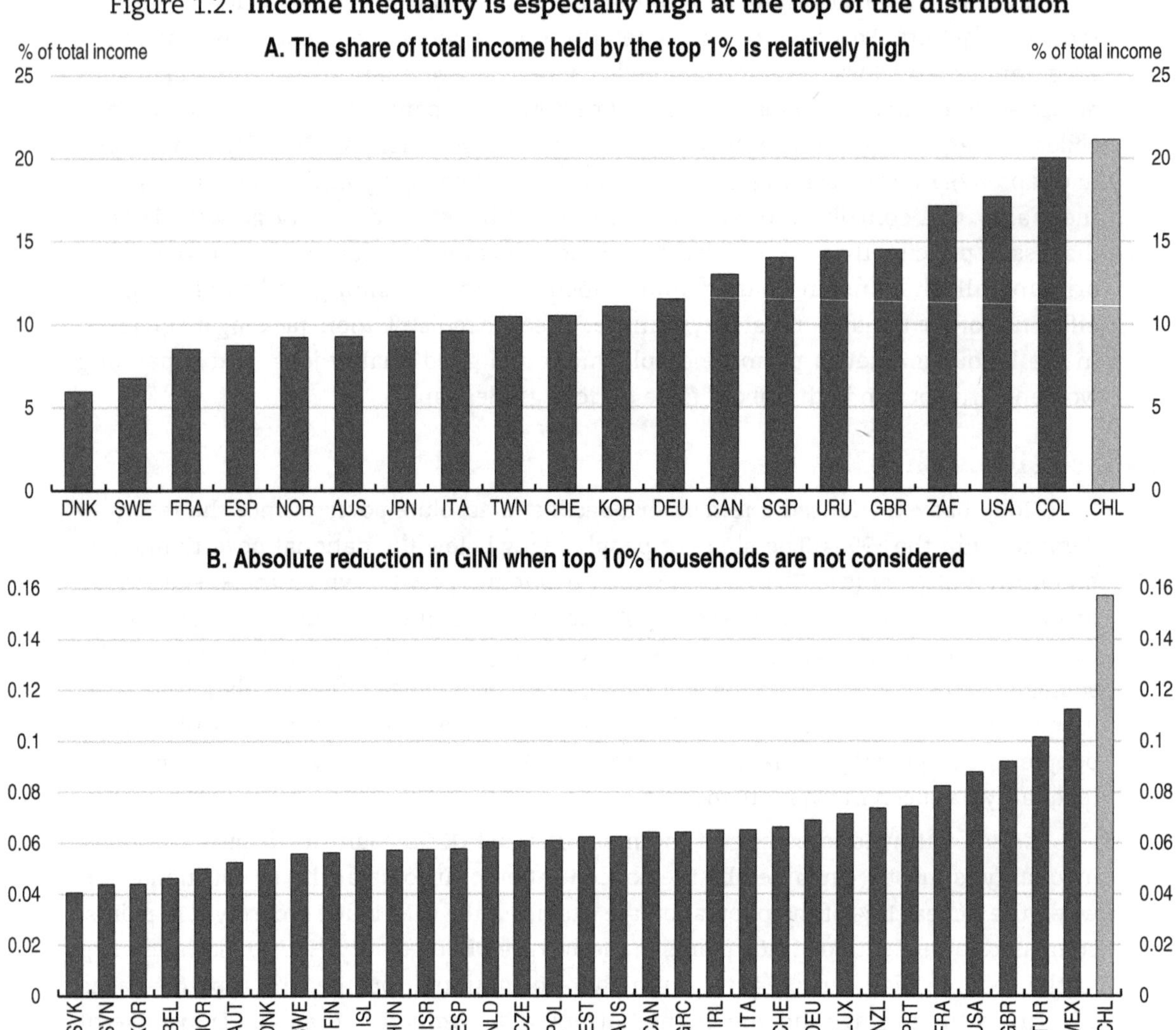

Source: Panel A: Lopez et al. (2013) for Chile and WTID for the rest of countries. Panel B: OECD estimations based on household surveys.

StatLink http://dx.doi.org/10.1787/888933302367

graduating from university by around four points and cuts the length of time children from poorer families spend in education by about half a year (OECD, 2015b). Furthermore, recent research finds consistent evidence that high inequality can put a significant brake on long-term growth, and that efforts to reduce it through redistribution – taxes and benefits – do not necessarily lead to slower growth (Ostry et al., 2014; Cingano, 2014; OECD, 2015b).

In Chile, like in other OECD countries, high income inequality is associated with low inter-generational social mobility (Figure 1.3, Panel A), as social status is passed on from parents to children (Corak, 2013). Statistical evidence compiled for this report show that this is also the case across Chilean regions (Box 1.1; Figure 1.3, Panel B). Being born in a high-income family can boost wages by more than 50% relative to the average, while a penalty of around 40% is expected when coming from a disadvantaged background. This is largely due to the transmission (or lack thereof) of human and social capital across generations: on average, 80% of individuals with at least one parent having attended university also have tertiary education (Chapter 2). In contrast, only 55% of individuals with parents with secondary education do so, and less than 13% among those with parents with primary

Figure 1.3. **Income inequality reflects inequality of opportunity**

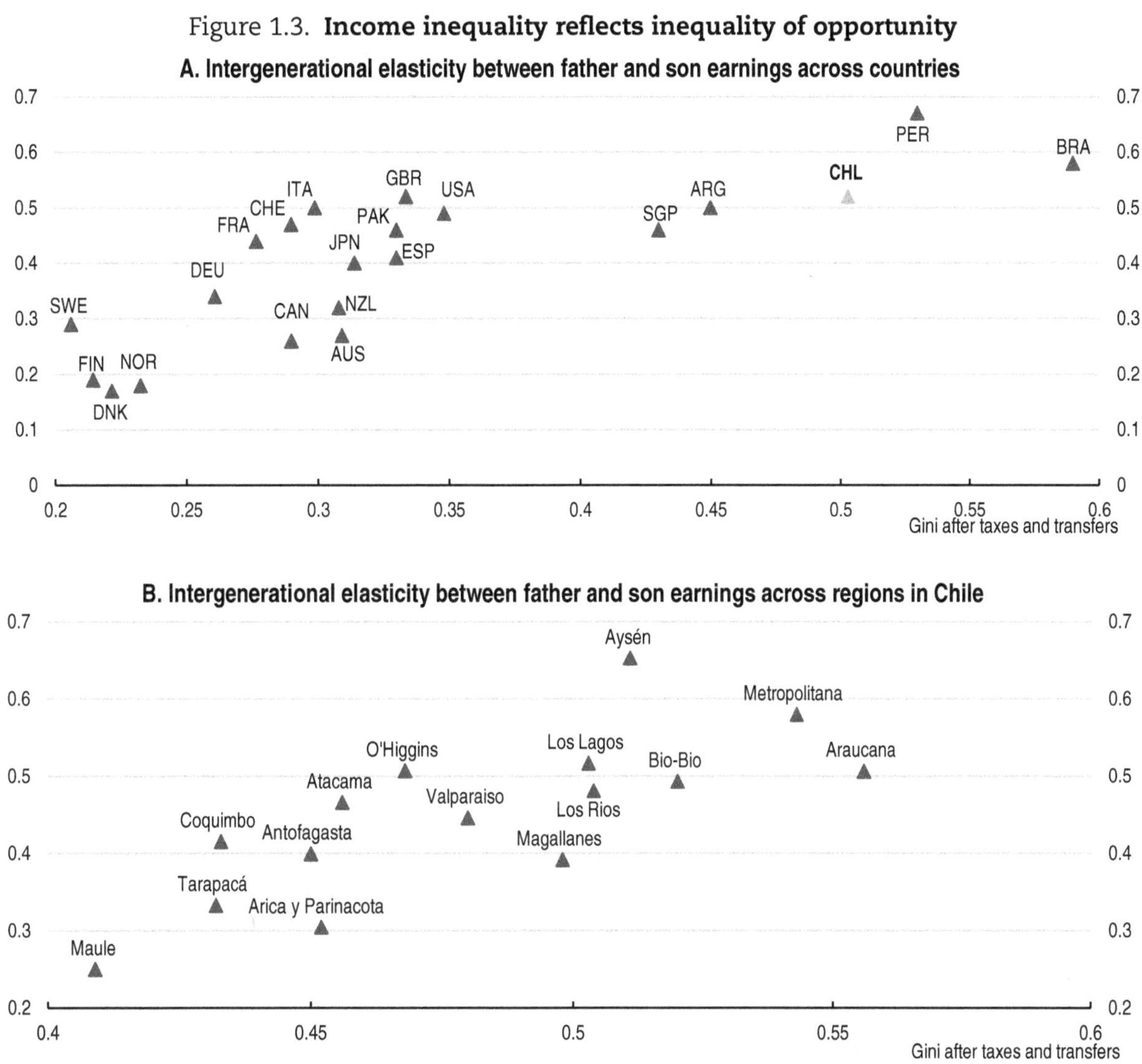

Source: OECD analysis based on CASEN 2013 and Corak (2013).

StatLink http://dx.doi.org/10.1787/888933302377

education or less. These social trends are even more pronounced at the very top of the ladder, a pattern characterised as "elite closure" (Torche, 2005; Nuñez and Miranda, 2011).

Low intergenerational income mobility is one of the most important indicators of individual income dynamics used in public policy discussions, as it can have important implications for political stability and economic growth (Corak, 2013). When the position people will occupy in society is determined by the position their parents had, people have low incentives to invest in their human capital or put effort to give the best of themselves, as they recognise this will not have any effect in their future relative incomes (Causa and Johansson, 2010). And lower investment in human capital can have a strong negative effect on productivity and growth (Heckman and Masterov, 2007; Chapter 2). Chile should focus on policies to increase intergenerational social mobility so that future incomes do not depend on parental socio-economic status, but on individual innate abilities and effort. When this happens people have a strong incentive to invest in their human capital, boosting productivity and growth, and reducing income inequality.

Box 1.1. **Intergenerational social mobility in Chile and its determinants**

The study of social mobility in developing countries is challenged by the lack of appropriate data covering two generations. In the case of Chile there is no available dataset including both parents' and children's income in their adulthood. Nevertheless, the survey *Encuesta de Caracterización Social y Económica* (CASEN, 2013) provides useful information about living conditions and asks respondents about the last educational level attended by their parents. Father's education can be used as a proxy of family background, as it is highly correlated with income and other traits that influence offspring's careers.

This box presents results from an experiment conducted for this Survey that measures the extent of intergenerational mobility by looking at the effect of father's education on individual's hourly wages once controlling for a set of demographic characteristics such as sex, age, marital status or location. The wage premium is the boost in wages associated with having a father who attended college instead of just medium education. Similarly, the wage penalty is the drop in wages associated with having a less educated father. Adding up the wage premium and wage penalty gives an overall measure of intergenerational wage mobility. The introduction of individuals' education as an additional explanatory factor allows distinguishing two distinctive channels of family influence. First, an indirect effect going through the transmission of education across generations. Second, a residual or direct effect linked to everything else not related to education like the transmission of genetics, social norms, contacts and so forth.

The main findings from this analysis are:

- Intergenerational mobility in Chile is low compared to other OECD countries (Figure 1.3, Panel A).
- Setting as the reference the average individual, having a father who went to university leads to a 60% increase in hourly wages. Likewise, having a father with basic or no education is associated with a 34% drop in wages.
- The measure of intergenerational mobility is very similar for men and women and across age cohorts. However, there are considerable regional differences (Figure 1.3, Panel B).
- There is a moderate relationship between income inequality and the measure of intergenerational mobility across regions. While the correlation with the direct effect is poor, the indirect effect due to transmission of education across generations is highly correlated with inequality (74%).

Exploiting differences in policy indicators across regions and employing interactions, this box also analysed the factors that explain the inequality-mobility relationship across regions, in particular the differences in social spending and the level of educational segregation. The results suggest that:

- A 10% increase in public educational spending in the 1990's (when the average individual was a teenager) is associated with up to a 9% decrease in the penalty of having a low educated father.
- Similarly, rising the percentage of students in public schools from 35% to 60% (e.g. from the level in Santiago Metropolitan to that in Los Lagos or Magallanes) could lead to a reduction of more than 30% in the influence of family income in the probability to attend college.

Evidence shows that the structure of income taxation and the size of transfers (e.g. unemployment benefits) affect the link between parental background and teenager cognitive skills and wages (Causa and Johansson, 2010). Therefore, improving redistributive and income support policies will not only help Chile reduce cross-sectional income inequality and poverty rates, it will also help increase intergenerational social mobility and provide more opportunities for all to invest in their human capital.

Improving the tax and welfare system

To reduce these social trends, Chile needs to increase the redistribution of income through the tax and transfer system, as little redistribution is taking place compared to other OECD countries (Figure 1.4), and several Latin American peers, like Argentina and Uruguay (Lustig, 2015). OECD evidence shows that in Chile transfers are more progressive than in the average OECD country (Joumard et al., 2012), and that this progressivity contributes to reducing the Gini after taxes and transfers. The problem is that the size of transfers is too small, thus limiting the impact of social programmes. Also, the narrow tax base, which greatly constrained public revenues, explains why the level of expenditures in public goods has been insufficient to reduce inequalities (Lopez and Miller, 2008).

Figure 1.4. **The tax and transfer system should do more to reduce inequality**

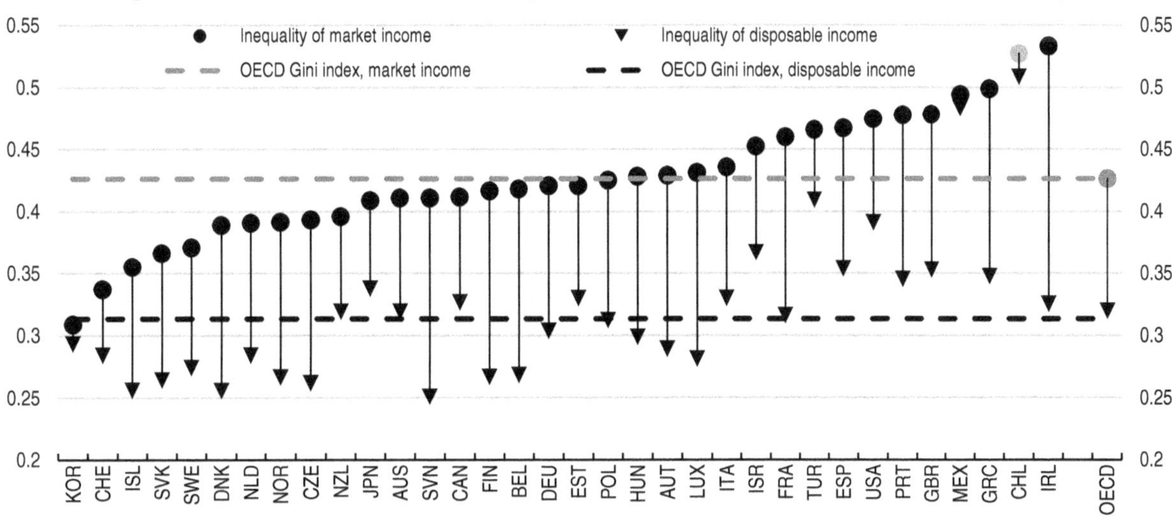

Note: The vertical access measure the percentage change in the Gini coefficient before and after taxes and transfers.
Source: OECD, *Income Distribution and Poverty Database*.

StatLink http://dx.doi.org/10.1787/888933302388

Raise more tax revenues

Chile's tax-to-GDP ratio (20.2%) is significantly lower than the OECD's average (33.7%) (Figure 1.5). Furthermore, Chile's tax revenues are lower than the tax revenues that most OECD countries were collecting when they had similar levels of GDP per capita. This suggests that there is scope to raise more tax revenues to meet growing public spending needs in education and health. To change this, the government has introduced a tax reform aimed at increasing general government revenues by 3 percentage points of GDP over the period 2015-18 (Box 1.2). The tax reform will reduce inequality as more than 75% of revenue increase will come from higher taxes on the top 1% (World Bank, 2015), eliminating tax expenditures and fighting tax evasion and avoidance.

Figure 1.5. **Public expenditure and tax revenue are very low**

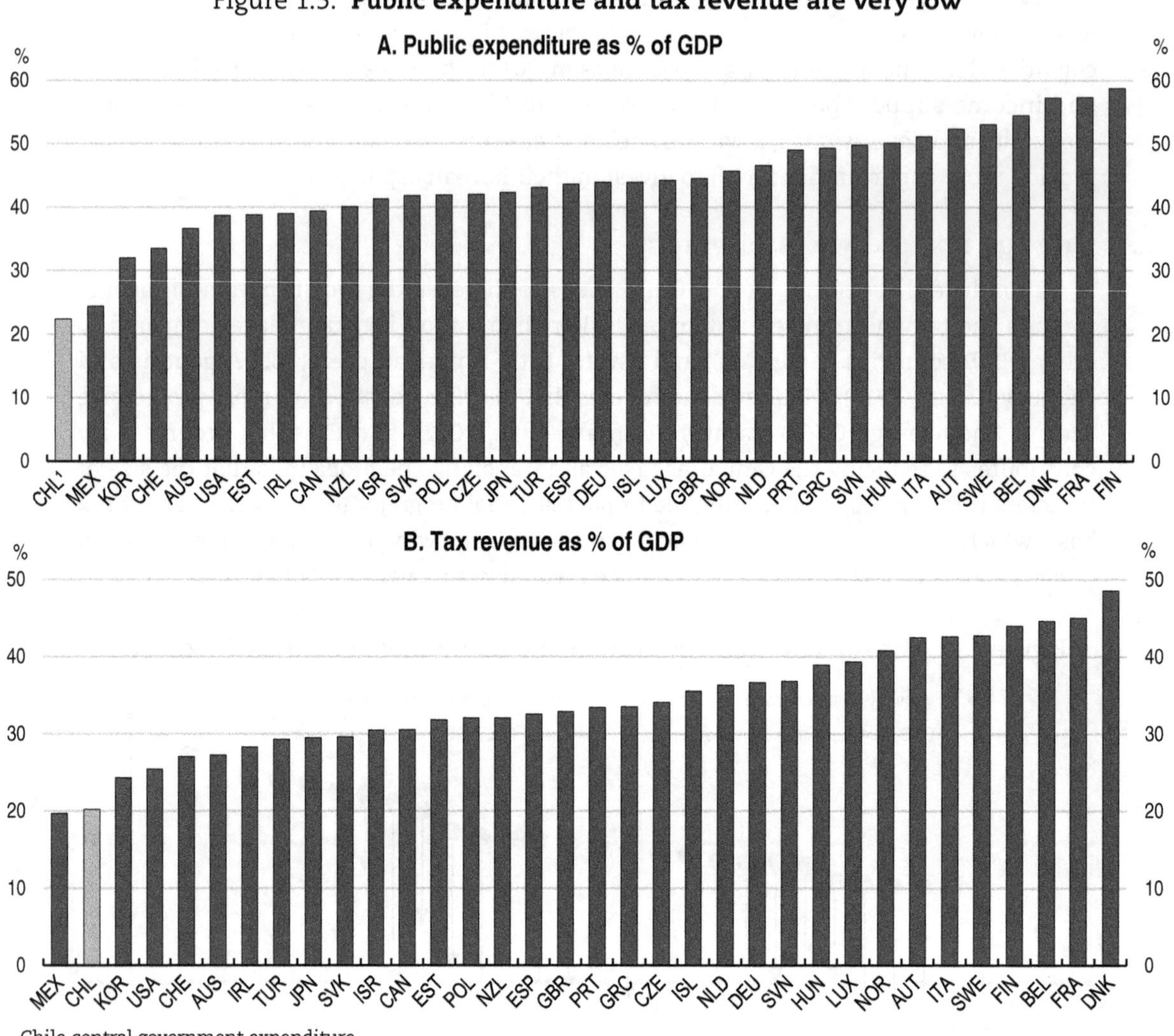

1. Chile central government expenditure.
Source: OECD, *National Accounts Statistics* and *Revenue Statistics 2014*.

StatLink http://dx.doi.org/10.1787/888933302395

Important tax exemptions mainly benefit higher-income earners and leave a large share of natural resource rents untaxed. In practice, evasion and avoidance by the top income earners is a significant contributor to the low impact of income taxes (Fairfield and Jorratt, 2015). Estimates show that just correcting for tax evasion makes a significant difference on the share of the income distribution (Lopez et al., 2015). In particular, the average participation of the top 1% on GDP over the period 2005-09 decreases by 2.5 percentage points of GDP.

A key component of the tax reform is a change to tax accrued profits whether or not they are distributed as dividends. This reform will increase revenues and has the potential to reduce inequality (Lopez et al., 2015). The reform could negatively affect investment and growth because it reduces after-tax returns on investment, however this could be compensated by a positive effect on long run growth through education, if the funding is used successfully in reforming the school system. Furthermore, there is some uncertainty about the revenue yield of the tax reform, stemming from how the private sector will

Box 1.2. **The 2014 tax reform**

In September 2014 the Chilean parliament passed an important tax reform. The law entered into force the last quarter of 2014, though some provisions will be phased in over the 2015-18 period. The overall goal tax reform is to raise the tax-to-GDP ratio to finance a large increase in education spending. The tax measures aim to raise an extra 3% of GDP. More than half of the increased revenues are forecasted to come from increased income taxation, mainly from corporate income (Table 1.1). Increases in compliance are forecast to increase revenues by 0.5% of GDP (17% of the overall reform revenue goal), while expansions in the VAT base will account for 0.3% of GDP (12% of the overall reform target. The law contains various provisions including:

- Extensive changes to corporate income tax (CIT).
- A reduction in the top PIT rate from 40 to 35%.
- Broadening of the base of VAT on real estate.
- Increases in health-related taxes.
- Increased taxation of carbon and other pollutants.
- Measures to improve compliance, reduce Base Erosion and Profit Shifting (BEPS), reduce evasion and avoidance.

Table 1.1. **Revenue projections from the 2014 tax reform**

	% of the projected revenue increase	% of GDP
Corporate income tax	48.30	1.46
Increase in collection due to plan to decrease tax evasion and avoidance	17.20	0.52
Taxing the sale of new properties and limiting the use of special VAT credit	11.90	0.36
Raising the stamp tax from 0.004 to 0.008	4.60	0.14
Change of tobacco tax	4.30	0.13
Other (Taxing capital income of real estate, restrictions on deemed income system, etc.)	3.60	0.11
Effect of the repeal of several measures	3.30	0.10
Fiscal traceability of specific taxes and mining tax auditing	2.60	0.08
New tax on source emissions (CO_2, NO_x, PM)	2.30	0.07
Effect tax change on alcoholic and non-alcoholic beverages	2.00	0.06
Historical FUT incentive	1.70	0.05
New tax on contaminating motor vehicles	1.70	0.05
Decrease in collection due to saving incentives and others	-3.60	-0.11
Total	**100**	**3.02**

adapt. The envisaged gradualism of implementation is thus welcome. It will remain important to monitor the effects on investment and savings and stand ready to adjust the reform if warranted.

Similarly, although it is clear that the reform will contribute to reduce inequality, the size of the effect is uncertain. For instance, estimates by the World Bank (World Bank, 2015) suggest that with the changes introduced by the tax reform, the share of net income received by the richest 1% of the population will fall by 1.1% of GDP. However, the effect of the reform on the Gini coefficient after taxes and transfers will be small (0.07 points). This is because the Gini coefficient is more sensitive to transfers to the centre of the distribution than to the tails, which is what this reform is targeting. These findings are consistent with previous research on the distributional effect – as measured by the Gini – of several changes in the tax structure in Chile (Engel et al., 1999; OECD, 2012a). These studies suggest that the targeting of expenditures and the level of the average tax rate are far more important determinants of income redistribution. Therefore, to boost the impact of redistribution system in reducing income inequality efforts should be strengthened to increase revenues by broadening the tax base and expand transfers.

To raise more revenues Chile could focus on broadening the tax base of the personal income tax (PIT), which does not contribute significantly to reduce inequality. The reform package did not address this key challenge. The PIT does not raise much revenue in Chile and one of the reasons is that many taxpayers do not have to pay the tax. This is in part because the tax-free income threshold is very high and higher PIT rates are only payable at very high income levels. An inclusive PIT reform would make significant changes in the PIT rate schedule, especially by lowering the bands at which the higher income rates are levied. In 2014, single taxpayers had to start paying PIT on gross earnings equivalent to 118% of the average wage. In contrast, taxpayers in the OECD on average had to start paying PIT on gross earnings equivalent to 29% of the average wage. Also the top PIT rate applies to very high income levels only. In 2014 in Chile, the top PIT rate of 40% had to be paid on gross earnings exceeding 12.7 times the average wage. After abolishing the top PIT bracket, this threshold in Chile will be lowered to 10.5 times the average wage, which remains very high. In comparison, the top PIT rate hits at 5.2 times the average wage on average across OECD countries in 2014 with a median value of 3.6 times the average wage. The PIT rate schedule in Chile is one of the least progressive rate schedules that can be found in the OECD. In Chile the average PIT rate increases very slowly per percentage point increase in the average wage over the 50% to 500% of the average wage income interval, taking into account tax allowances, deductions, credits and PIT rates. Low values indicate that the average PIT rate hardly changes when income rises on average over that interval.

Similarly, the generous deductions for private pension savings and mortgage interest deductions could be cut significantly to increase revenues and reduce inequality. The additional tax revenues raised could be used to provide more generous benefits for particular families, either through direct cash benefits or indirect PIT reliefs, including for lower income families with children. In Chile, only "Single Taxpayers at 167% of the average wage" have to pay a small amount of PIT; single parents can benefit from a small child benefit, which reduces the tax burden slightly below 7%. Chile has very generous non-standard tax reliefs which primarily benefit richer taxpayers, which contributes to lowering the PIT system's progressivity. Chile allows taxpayers to deduct voluntary contributions and voluntary pension fund savings from taxable income; the maximum deduction in 2014 (CLP 14 776 260) was more than twice the average wage. Chile also has a very generous mortgage interest relief deduction.

Finally, reducing informality is a key challenge to increase revenues, with significant implications for tax policy. The level of informality – as measured by the share of people not contributing to social security – in Chile, although low for Latin American standards, is high compared to other OECD countries. There are many reasons why broadening the tax net to informal operators should be a priority: it would not only raise additional revenues, it would also restore equity between formal taxpayers and informal operators, raise social welfare as workers employed in the informal sector have limited access to social protection, and ultimately boost economic growth as productivity in the informal sector tends to be lower than in the formal sector. The tax system can affect individuals' decisions to move out of the informal sector through a combination of positive incentives (e.g. lowering the tax burden on low-income earners, simplification of tax procedures) and dissuasive measures (e.g. stronger audit capacity and sanctions).

Create a more inclusive pension system

In most OECD countries, pensions explain a large share of the overall redistributive impact of the tax and transfer system (OECD, 2012a). In Chile, however, pensions do not help to reduce inequality, as the Gini coefficient before and after pension contributions are very similar (Lustig, 2015). In 2008 Chile undertook reform to improve pension coverage and safety net benefits as part of their efforts to fight poverty in old age more effectively. As a result Chile's old-age pension system has reduced elderly poverty from around 23% in 2008 to 20% in 2011, thanks to this reform that introduced a solidarity pension. However, the average pension remain modest among other things because they are mostly financed by mandatory contributions that remain low (10% of earnings – compared to 20% on average across the OECD). In Chile low earners' pension benefits replacement rate is only between 50% and 60% of their pre-retirement earnings, among the lowest rates in the OECD (Figure 1.6). This means retirees will face a significantly lower standard of living than the one they had during their working lives.

Figure 1.6. **Net replacement rates for full-career workers are relatively low**

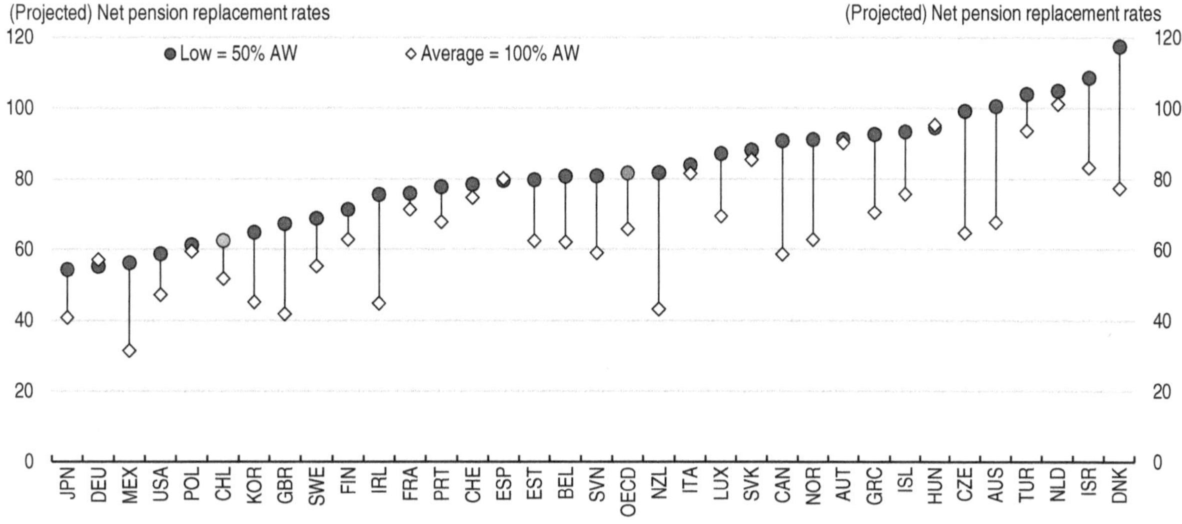

Note: "Average" and "low" earnings levels refer to 100% AW and 50% of the AW respectively.
Source: OECD, *Pension at a Glance Database.*

StatLink http://dx.doi.org/10.1787/888933302408

In 2011, Chile ushered in the last phase of its 2008 reform to cover 60% of the poorest elderly people in its public solidarity pension system (SPS), a new pillar that provides means-tested benefits to those who receive no, or very little, pension. People are entitled to the solidarity pillar if they have accumulated insufficient assets in their mandatory defined contribution plan to give them a retirement income above a certain income threshold. However, actual data by the Chilean Superintendence of Pensions shows a take-up rate of 43% since the new solidarity pillar was introduced in 2008. People may not be claiming their solidarity benefits because of a lack of knowledge, although the Chilean authorities argue that the population has been widely informed when the new solidarity pillar was introduced.

In Chile basic pensions become available to men at the age of 65 (same as OECD average) and to women at the age of 60 (OECD average of 64). In Chile, self-employed workers have been allowed to contribute voluntarily to the pension system, but have not been covered by any mandatory pension scheme. In most OECD countries, self-employed workers have mandatory social protection coverage. In most countries, they are covered by the same pension scheme as employees (e.g. Canada, Hungary and Korea). In other countries, self-employed workers contribute to separate special pension schemes (e.g. Austria, Belgium and France). Some countries provide preferential tax treatment for social contributions to the self-employed to extend social protection coverage. Although in Chile mandatory contributions of self-employed were expected to start in 2016, it is under discussion a proposal to implement it gradually since 2018.

The Chilean government set up an expert commission (*Comisión Asesora Presidencial sobre el Sistema de Pensiones*) to assess the pension system, identifying its strengths and limitations, and elaborate a set of remedies (Bravo et al., 2015). The commission examined a wide range of issues, but focused particularly on the large number of future pensioners who have low contribution densities and low replacement rate that the pension system have. Overall, half of men have contribution densities lower than 47.5%, and half of women have densities of less than 12.8%. These low contribution are associated with work histories that include periods of self-employment, informal employment, unemployment or professional inactivity, and are particularly a problem for women and individuals in low income brackets.

The recommendations of the commission will be examined by a special council of minister which will analyse which of the different recommendations could be implemented. Some of the recommendations of the expert commission are highly consistent with OECD best practices. To make the pension system more sustainable and improve replacement rates, the required contribution rates should be gradually raised from 10% to 14%. In addition, to make the system more inclusive, reforms could focus on increasing the level of the solidarity pension (available to the bottom 60% of households), to improve replacement rates, notably for women and the poor. The reform should increase the statutory retirement age, equalising the retirement age of men and women at 65 years, and periodically review the retirement age to be consistent with life expectancy. These features are a key feature of sustainable pension systems. The reform should also remove the modality of programmed retirement pension to avoid decreasing pensions over time, and encourage annuitisation.

Strengthen cash transfer programmes for the most vulnerable populations

The redistributive power of income taxes and cash benefits for the working-age population is limited, in part, because the size of the transfers are low (Figure 1.7). Poor families can draw on the *Ingreso Etico Familiar* (IEF), a group of cash transfers aimed at improving the living conditions of extremely poor families. The IEF includes a basic benefit (*Bono por Dignidad*) plus a series of conditional cash transfers related to medical check-ups of children, and school- attendance and results. Relevant payment rates are low when compared to other OECD countries, as the basic benefit amounts to less than USD 30 per month and slightly over USD 10 per child per month for other payments such as the school attendance bonus. These benefits are important to extremely poor families, but not all such families receive support: 60.6% of the families in receipt of the IEF belong to the 3 lowest income deciles, but only 8.8% of the families in the lowest decile received such support.

Figure 1.7. **Public spending on cash benefits for family are very low**

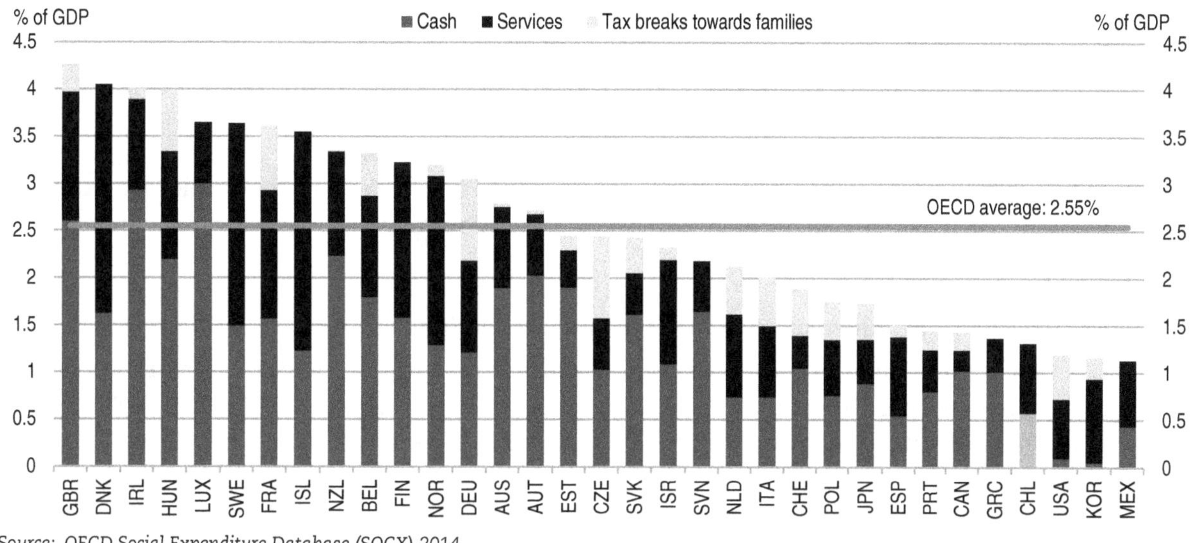

Source: OECD Social Expenditure Database (SOCX) 2014.

StatLink http://dx.doi.org/10.1787/888933302416

In monetary terms the *Bono al Trabajo de la Mujer* (working women subsidy), is the most important component of the IEF. To be eligible women must be between 25 and 59 years old, work in the formal sector, earn less, as most women do, than CLP 423 685 per month (USD 689, the average wage is around USD 950 per month) and belong to the 40% most vulnerable group of the population as defined, among other factors, by the *Ficha de Protección Social* (FPS). At least 40% of poorest working women could be in receipt for the working women subsidy. However, in 2015, the average number of recipients was 280 000 who received less than USD 100 per month.

The FPS is a key tool used by the authorities to determine access to means-tested cash transfers and in-kind benefits. Completion of the list of questions in the FPS provides the authorities with a profile of (low-income) households. The tool aims to measure long-term household income capacity as based on the households' housing and living conditions, location, family situation, health, education, income and employment, which are somehow weighted into an overall score that affects access to social support. The FPS has been criticised for its complexity and lack of transparency. Moreover, increasing its focus on current income stream may help better target support for low-income households. Changes in FPS are being implemented, and should be effective already in 2016. Under the new system only actual incomes will be considered, people will be still asked to enter a register, as in the current FPS, and these records will be matched with administrative records of income.

Strengthening these poverty alleviation policies as planned by the government is welcome, but additional spending will be necessary to effectively fight poverty. Efforts should focus on vulnerable groups, like children, elderly and minority groups which are overly represented among the lowest deciles of the income distribution. An example of the latter are the indigenous populations, which in Chile represent around 9.1% of the total population (Casen, 2013). Although poverty rates for indigenous population have decreased over recent decades thanks to special initiatives targeted to them, they are still overrepresented in the lowest deciles of the income distribution, and experience higher poverty rates (23.4%) than the non-indigenous population (13.5%). In rural areas, indigenous peoples have little land and tend to be concentrated in extreme fragile, rapidly deteriorating environments. In urban areas, particularly in large urban centres such as Santiago, Concepción and Temuco, indigenous peoples are clustered in the poorest neighbourhoods, with limited access to social services, and a significant proportion of the population is underemployed or work in the informal sector. Indigenous peoples struggle to find labour opportunities because of racial discrimination. Indeed, evidence shows that in Chile the effect of class is more important in determining earnings than academic performance (Nuñez and Gutierrez, 2004).

Enhance fiscal equalisation to reduce regional inequalities

Chile should enhance fiscal equalisation across municipalities, as they differ strongly in resources and capacity to provide education and social programmes (OECD, 2015c). The main source of municipal income is property taxes, which penalises municipalities with a lot of low-value houses. Revenue per capita of the richest decile of municipalities is more than twice as high as those of the poorest decile even after fiscal equalisation. Within Greater Santiago the three richest municipalities have five times more resources per inhabitant than the three poorest ones. The Gini coefficient for average per capita fiscal revenues by decile also suggests that fiscal disparities across municipalities are high in Chile and fiscal equalisation does relatively little to correct this. Poorer municipalities need stronger resources to provide their citizens with high-quality services that help them overcome poverty and reduce income inequalities.

The government has launched an ambitious set of legal reforms to implement a "decentralisation and development agenda" to address disparities via better adaptation of public policies to regional and local needs and opportunities. The legislative proposals concern three main pillars: i) a constitutional reform allowing the election of the regional *intendentes* (keeping a *gobernador* as representative of the central power); ii) the transfer of competences and in the following areas: economic development, social development, infrastructure and housing to the regions; and iii) changes to the laws on regional financing and fiscal responsibility. In addition, the authorities have formulated special plans for four "extreme" regions that are geographically very remote – Aysén, Magallanes, Arica and Los Lagos (province of Palena and commune of Cochamó). These provide for substantial new investment resources and include greater flexibility to define targets and standards locally. However, they also raise capacity-building and absorption challenges for the regions concerned.

Reducing inequalities in the labour market

There are limits, however, to what the tax-and-transfer can do and the availability of well-paid jobs also has a major role to play in reducing inequality. Evidence shows that income inequality before taxes and transfers reflect mainly differences in labour market outcomes, as they accounts for around 75% of household income inequality across OECD countries, much more than the 25% accounted by self-employment and capital income combined (Figure 1.8). Over the past two decades, job gains have driven unemployment sharply down and encouraged many persons to participate in the labour market. However, the Chilean labour market remains segmented. Many poor workers do not have a labour contract and therefore do not have access to health insurance and unemployment benefits. This makes them extremely vulnerable and at risk of falling into

Figure 1.8. **Labour income inequality is the main contributor to household market income inequality**

As measured by the Gini coefficient

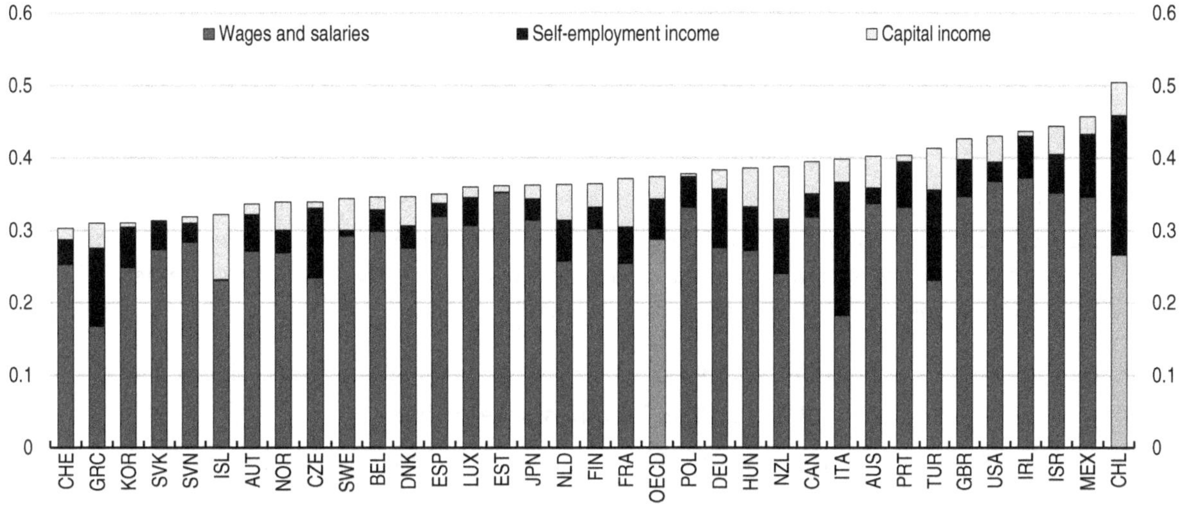

Note: Contributions to overall household market income inequality are derived by multiplying the concentration coefficients of each income source by their weight in total market income.
Source: OECD (2012a).

StatLink http://dx.doi.org/10.1787/888933302422

poverty. Many workers also have non-standard jobs (temporary contracts, part-time schedules, etc.). Indeed, the share of temporary workers is the largest in the OECD (OECD, 2015a).

Update labour legislation to help reduce inequality

Some of the countervailing forces and labour market institutions that favour redistribution in Chile, principally unions, collective bargaining mechanisms and statutory minimum wages, exist but have a limited reach. In particular, collective bargaining strength in the private sector remains weak. Although the percentage of contracts that are negotiated through collective bargaining has risen since 2001, only 11% of all contracts were collectively bargained in 2011. Collective bargaining in Chile has significant levels of decentralisation and fragmentation, where negotiation occurs at the level of the firm, but in contrast to similar cases such as in Japan for example, in Chile the co-ordination is particularly weak.

Labour relations in Chile are governed by the Labour Code which has its origins in a 1979 reform. Although the Labour Code recognises the rights of workers to organise, a number of restrictions were placed upon organizing. The right to strike was severely limited by procedural rules and a right to lock-out was granted to employers (Reinecke and Valenzuela, 2011). Currently, two different types of collective bargaining co-exist: one with the right to strike, and the other without the right to strike. It is this last category that has grown during the last 20 years (to almost 31.4% of the total of workers covered by collective bargaining). Furthermore, those workers who do have the right to strike can be replaced from the first day of the strike under certain conditions. As a result the power of unions and collective bargaining mechanisms has been greatly reduced.

Unionisation density and coverage are relatively low in Chile, and strongly concentrated in the public sector. Improving social dialogue and industrial relations in Chile can be important elements of a more equitable and inclusive growth. The labour reform (*Proyecto de Modernización de Relaciones Laborales*; *Ministerio Secretaría General de la Presidencia*, 2014) currently in discussion in the Senate, aims at expanding the coverage and scope of collective bargaining by empowering trade unions and by bringing collective bargaining processes closer to other OECD countries, in particular European. The reform has a number of major provisions that change the bargaining conditions for collective agreements (Box 1.3). Among these provisions, it is likely that the change in the right to bargain collectively, which after the reform will be restricted only to union members, and the change in the extension of benefits, which now will occur only under the agreement of unions and employer, will increase union membership.

Box 1.3. **The labour market reform**

The labour reform (*Proyecto de Modernización de Relaciones Laborales*) currently in discussion in the Senate aims at expanding the coverage and scope of collective bargaining. The most important areas of the reform are:

1. *Right to bargain:* Currently non-union groups can negotiate collectively in the presence of unions. The reform proposes that unions have the priority for collective negotiations in the companies where they exist. Non-union members will only be able to bargain collectively by affiliating to the union in firms where unions exist. In firm where there are no unions, groups will still be allowed to exist.
2. *Level of collective negotiation:* Collective negotiation remains at the firm level.
3. *Extension of the benefits of collective agreement:* Currently, employers can unilaterally extend the benefits to non-union workers and workers' pay 75% of union members' fee. The reform proposes that the union and the employer should agree whether the benefits are extended, and to benefit non-union members will have to pay the full union member fee.
4. *Coverage of collective negotiations:* Workers on apprenticeship and temporary contracts, which are currently excluded from negotiations, will be allowed to negotiate with some restrictions.
5. *Adaptability pacts:* Currently companies and worker can arrange special work conditions with the approval of the *Direccion del Trabajo* (DT). The reform will allow negotiations of special work conditions, without going through the DT, if the company has 30% affiliation in one or more unions.
6. *Right to strike:* Employers will no longer be allowed to replace workers on strike, and unions will have to provide necessary personnel to comply with indispensable operations.
7. *Minimum period to start negotiations:* The minimum period is reduced to six months for new large firms. The negotiation process starts with a floor: the employer cannot offer lower benefits than the ones that already exist, with some exclusions.
8. *Gender issues:* The reform proposes to make mandatory the incorporation of women in the bargaining commissions for bargaining collectively and requires firms to provide information about gender gaps in wages.

Estimates produced for this Survey using household data from the National Socioeconomic Characterization Survey (CASEN), suggest that increasing union membership will have a stronger and significant effect for middle income households than for lower income households, and specially than the top income deciles (Figure 1.9), mainly because those affiliated to unions today belong to sixth and higher quintile. Therefore, the effect on overall income distribution is ambiguous. However, the fact that income inequality is larger at the top of the distribution indicates that the Gini coefficient will be reduced.

Figure 1.9. **The effect of increasing union membership would be stronger for middle income households**

Effect on log earnings of raising the share of workers affiliated to a union by 1 percentage point

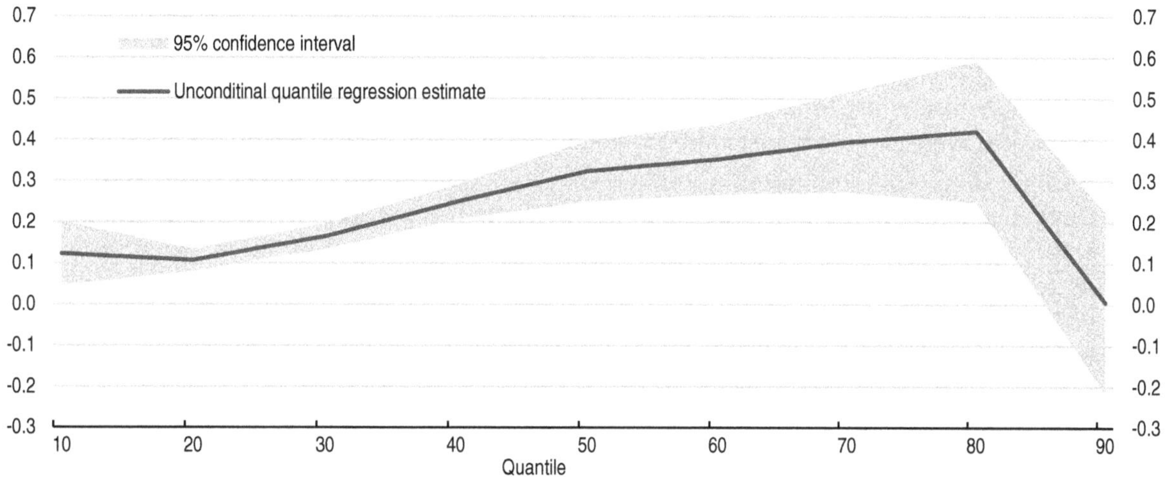

Note: Unconditional quantile depression estimates for employed individuals using data from the National Socioeconomic Characterization Survey (CASEN).

Source: OECD estimates using CASEN (2013) following the methodology of Fournier and Koske (2012).

StatLink http://dx.doi.org/10.1787/888933302435

As a major component of the rules that govern a modern economy, the reform to the Labour Code should also pay special attention to the details and be taken as an opportunity to make changes that also address other pressing challenges in the Chilean labour market. For instance, the change in the right to strike is a right step forward to protect workers' rights. But it should be balanced by clearly defining the range of minimum services that are guaranteed in the case of strikes. An option could be to clearly define some exemptions to the prohibition of replacement by defining specific jobs or tasks for which a replacement during strike may occur. Similarly, the proposed change in the extension of benefits of collective agreement should be reconsidered, as it may create the possibility of having two workers in the firm with similar tasks and experience who earn different wages, which goes against the goal of reducing inequalities in the labour market.

The reform should also consider adjusting employment protection legislation, which is relatively high for regular contracts producing incentives for firms to hire under non-regular work arrangements, thus resulting in labour-market duality (OECD, 2015b). Protection for workers from individual dismissal is among the highest in the OECD, with high severance pay for workers having at least 4 years of tenure. Although the changes to the collective bargaining may bring enhanced protection to workers in specific firms, given that negotiation will not be carried out at the sectoral or industry level, they are unlikely to change the indicator of employment protection (Venn, 2009).

Focus on protecting workers rather than jobs

Current legislation provides strong protection for employees with indefinite contracts, while providing little security to workers in non-standard contracts. Evidence shows that this strongly increases the level of inequality (OECD, 2011a). Non-standard employment is associated with poorer labour conditions (wages, working time, job security, leave entitlements, etc.). In Chile, workers with lower level of education are overrepresented in temporary employment, as are workers in small firms (OECD, 2012a). Similarly, households with temporary work arrangements are overrepresented at the lower end of the household income distribution.

Temporary workers are worse off in terms of many aspects of job quality. They tend to receive less training and, in addition, have more job strain and have less job security than workers in standard jobs. Earnings levels are also lower in terms of annual and hourly wages. Evidence shows that temporary workers in OECD countries face a wage penalty, even after controlling for observable individual, family and work characteristics (OECD, 2015a). On average, a temporary contract worker receives an hourly wage that is 11% lower for men than their counterparts in standard jobs (13% lower for women). The under-investment in human capital associated with short-term contracts can give rise to lower wages for temporary workers. While the wages of temporary workers increase with age and skill level, they grow more slowly than those of standard workers. As a result, the wage differences between temporary and standard workers tend to widen with age or skill. This implies that years of labour market experience may not be valued in the same way for temporary workers as for standard workers.

Furthermore, across OECD countries temporary work tends to lower wages at the bottom of the earnings distribution, while the effect is often neutral at the top, thereby contributing to increased individual earnings inequality. And Chile is no exemption. Evidence shows that earnings gaps between permanent and temporary workers are significantly larger at the bottom of the wage distribution (the so-called sticky-floor effect) (Bosio, 2014; Santangelo, 2011). As a result, a high share of temporary workers contributes to the wide overall wage inequality, since it increases inequality at the bottom end of the distribution and has a neutral effect on wage inequality at the top end.

Temporary contracts can provide workers an entry-way to firms to then transition into regular contracts providing more job security. Temporary contracts provide employers with a mechanism to test workers before making a stronger commitment and adjust to business cycles by not renewing temporary contracts when business is slow. However, across the OECD and especially in Chile, many workers do not transition to indefinite contracts and firms abuse temporary contracts. These workers cycle between temporary contracts, with unemployment spells in between (limiting their social and health contributions and their income security) and resulting in large turnover within firms.

To rebalance job protection, Italy has introduced a single standard contract applying only to new employment contracts, with employment protection increasing with tenure (Box 1.4). This new contract provides a basic level of protection for the first two years, after which the level of compensation for unfair dismissal increases. As evidence becomes available about the benefits, and possible costs of the single contract in Italy, Chile could usefully draw lessons. Increasing the share of permanent workers can help Chile reduce income inequality. Estimates produced for this Survey using household data from the National Socioeconomic Characterization Survey (CASEN) suggest that if temporary

Box 1.4. **The Italian labour market reform: Single contracts**

In Italy, a new open-ended contract has been in place since March 2015, as part of the Jobs Act, a package of labour market reforms introduced by the Renzi administration. This new contract increases employment protection with the job tenure, aiming at simplifying and streamlining dismissal rules while reducing labour market dualism. This new contract is applied only to new employment contracts, grandfathering existing rights. The temporary contracts will be transformed into open-ended ones by 2016, unless collective agreements set flexibility criteria for the use of temporary contracts.

This new open-ended contract limits the possibility of reinstatement of workers following unfair dismissal, excluding this possibility for redundancy dismissal ("*motivo oggettivo*", due to production and technological factors in the firm). In this arrangement, unfairly dismissed workers will receive monetary compensation which is increasing with the tenure. The monetary compensation will be equal to 2 monthly wages per year of service (with a minimum amount equivalent to 4 months and a maximum amount equivalent to 24 monthly wages). It preserves the right of reinstatement in case of invalid and discriminatory dismissals (because of race, gender, religion or disability) and for very specific cases of unfair disciplinary dismissals.

The Jobs Act reduces legal risk associated with unfair dismissal provisions which have been identified as most burdensome and affecting gross worker flows in general (OECD, 2013). By increasing predictability and thus lowering the effective costs of dismissal (i.e. even if judged to be unfair by courts, the subsequent financial costs are foreseen), the Jobs Act encourages firms to create more jobs.

There still remains some stringency on the definition of fair/unfair dismissal and compensation following unfair dismissal. In the case of redundancy, dismissal is judged as unfair if a transfer and/or a retraining to adapt the worker to different work is not attempted prior to dismissal ("*repechage*"); compensation following unfair dismissal is equivalent to 24 months of salary for a worker at 20 years of tenure against the OECD average of 6 months.

The Jobs Act also introduced a new form of out-of-court procedure, applying to all dismissal cases. According to this procedure, the employer pays the worker an indemnity equal to 1 monthly wage per year of service (with a minimum amount equivalent to 2 monthly wages and a maximum amount equivalent to 18 monthly wages), which is not subject to social contribution or fiscal taxation. This compensation could be considered as similar in some respects to severance pay. The acceptance of this transaction prevents any further dispute by the worker, that is, appealing to courts for a dismissal to be unfair or not.

Source: OECD (2015), *OECD Economic Surveys: Italy 2015*.

contracts are reduced by 10% relative to permanent contracts, earnings of the lowest income deciles will increase by around 3% more than income of the highest incomes deciles (Figure 1.10). Therefore, well designed labour reform that increases the share of permanent workers in Chile could have significant effects reducing income inequalities.

Efficient activation policies to improve labour opportunities for the less advantageous

Youth in Chile face a high risk of unemployment. Lack of job-specific skills needed in the labour market, low levels of general skills, absence of work experience programmes, and low coverage of financial incentives for employers to hire and train youth may hinder young workers' employability. The OECD Action Plan for Youth recommends a set of

Figure 1.10. **Reducing the share of temporary contracts can reduce earnings inequality**

Effect on log earnings from reducing by 1% the share of temporary contracts relative to permanent contracts

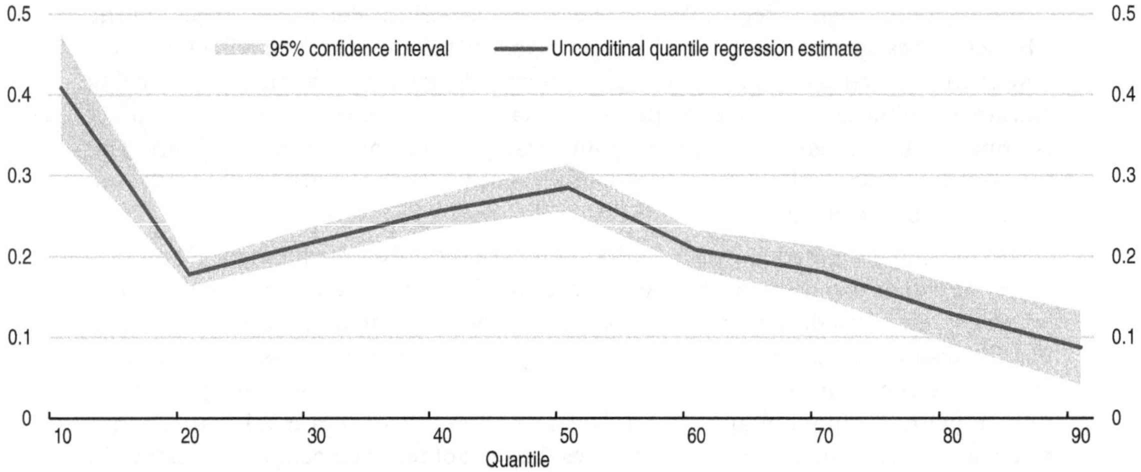

Note: Unconditional quantile regression estimate for employed individuals using data from the National Socioeconomic Characterization Survey (CASEN).

Source: OECD estimates using CASEN (2013) following the methodology of Fournier and Koske (2012),

StatLink http://dx.doi.org/10.1787/888933302444

measures, including active labour market strategies and encouraging employers to expand quality apprenticeships or internship programmes, while strengthening the education system, the role and effectiveness of Vocational Education and Training and assisting the transition from school to work. The Chilean government is supporting youth employability along some of these lines. The public employment service (*Servicio Nacional de Capacitación y Empleo*, SENCE), specifically targets youth in its training provision. The *Subsidio al Empleo Joven* and the *Subsidio Previsional a los Trabajadores Jóvenes* are attempts to lower employment costs for youth in the formal sector. *MásCapaz* is an ambitious worker training programme to bring youth and women closer to the labour market which during 2015, the first year of full scale implementation, has attracted 56 thousand to training course, with 50% being younger than 30 years and 75.8% belonging to the 20% of the poorest. Also *Yo Trabajo*, run by FOSIS, is an attempt to target low-skilled individuals and those in the margins of the labour market. *MásCapaz* training schemes are long durations, they have between 200 and 300 hours.

However, more efforts are required. In particular, the government could strengthen the public employment service's job-search support, improve the linkages between upper secondary and tertiary education and employer needs, and offer guidance counselling services and work experience programmes beginning in lower- or upper-secondary schools and continuing through the public employment service. Developing an apprenticeship system and enhancing the work-based component in vocational education and training (VET) and terminal programmes would also improve youth's employability. In addition, more and better incentives could be provided for employers to hire and train youth by facilitating and expanding the take-up of youth employment subsidies so that more SMEs benefit (OECD, 2010).

More generally, Chile should invest more resources to improve worker training and lifelong learning system, which is currently ineffective and does not benefit workers and firms that need it most. Currently the training system is mostly based on tax credits to employers that mainly benefits large employers, leaving low-skilled or low-income workers and SMEs, who could benefit the most, out. In addition, training schemes are usually ineffective due to their short duration and quality varies widely (Larrañaga et al., 2014). Training and adult skill development more generally need to be better linked to the labour market. Following the example of other OECD countries, Chile should systematically assess current or future skill needs (OECD, 2015d). Doing job training right can boost productivity of workers because it facilitates the use of goods and work tools that require more technical skills, accelerates the process of adoption of new technologies and helps individuals to engage in sectors high productivity.

Finally, Chile should increase spending on active labour market policies, which is currently 0.36% of GDP, significantly lower than the average country in the OCDE or 1.37% of GDP (Figure 1.11). Both SENCE and the *Oficinas Municipales de Intermediación Laboral* (OMILs) need to increase their capacity to deliver high quality counselling, guidance, job-search assistance and training based on workers' needs; all of which are key to help the unemployed find stable work. The planned extension of the training system to the unemployed and vulnerable workers through the public employment service will reduce the inequalities in access to worker training. The new auction of the *Bolsa Nacional de Empleo* (BNE) is a step in that direction; however, it should be integrated with training opportunities. Efforts to further reform SENCE may increase its ability to deal with its ambitious mandate of co-ordinating worker training and activation policies and the addition of quality assurance requirements to training providers may increase the efficacy of worker training.

Figure 1.11. **Spending in active labour market policies is very low**

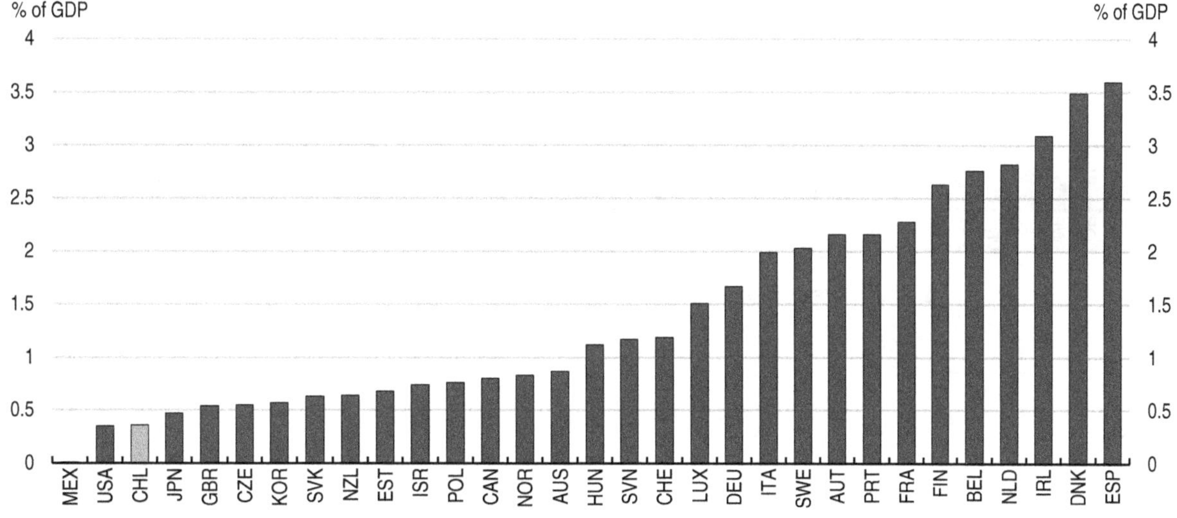

Note: The figure for Chile does not include the recent programme *MasCapaz*, which will increase spending on labour market policies by 0.4% of GDP.
Source: *OECD Employment and Labour Market Statistics 2014.*

StatLink http://dx.doi.org/10.1787/888933302304

Ongoing efforts to promote the development of Sector Skills Councils, the development of qualification frameworks and occupational standards will facilitate the linkages between skills development and skill needs. To strengthen its system to inform skills policy based on current and future skill needs strong social partner organisations (e.g. Sector Skills Councils that include SMEs) are needed and partnerships between workers, employers and training institutions need to be developed, together with the public employment service's role in co-ordinating training that meets labour market and reaches those workers and sectors that need it most. In addition, occupational standards and qualification frameworks have to be developed and used effectively. While the efforts put forth by *ChileValora* to develop occupational standards are very welcome, they are insufficient. Rigorous and continuous methods to assess and anticipate skill needs are also needed, together with methods for quality assurance and the monitoring of training providers.

Closing gender gaps

Female labour force participation in Chile has increased significantly since the mid-1990s, but it is still low at 54% in 2011 compared with an OECD average of 62%, and the gap with men is among the widest in the OECD (Figure 1.12, Panel A). The share of women on board of listed companies in Chile is among the lowest in the OECD (Figure 1.12, Panel B). The major obstacle Chilean women face to participate more fully is the traditional gender roles towards work and care. At home, Chilean women spend 4 hours per day more

Figure 1.12. **Women face all kind of inequalities**

A. Gender gap in labour force participation is high

B. The share of women on the boards of listed companies is low

Source: Panel A: *OECD Employment and Labour Market Statistics 2014*. Panel B: World Values Survey Association 2009.

StatLink http://dx.doi.org/10.1787/888933302458

on unpaid work than men (OECD, 2012b). Unlike other OECD countries, the gender pay gap in Chile is mainly explained by the characteristic of jobs occupied by women (Figure 1.13). Women dominate the service sector (83% of women, compared to 34% of men), in particular the sectors of health and social work, followed by education. Women often work part-time or drop out of the labour force after childbearing. Together with low earnings, this increases the risk of old age poverty: 60% of women affiliated with the pension system have contributed for less than 50% of the time than men.

Figure 1.13. **Differences in the type of job explain most of the gender pay gap in Chile**

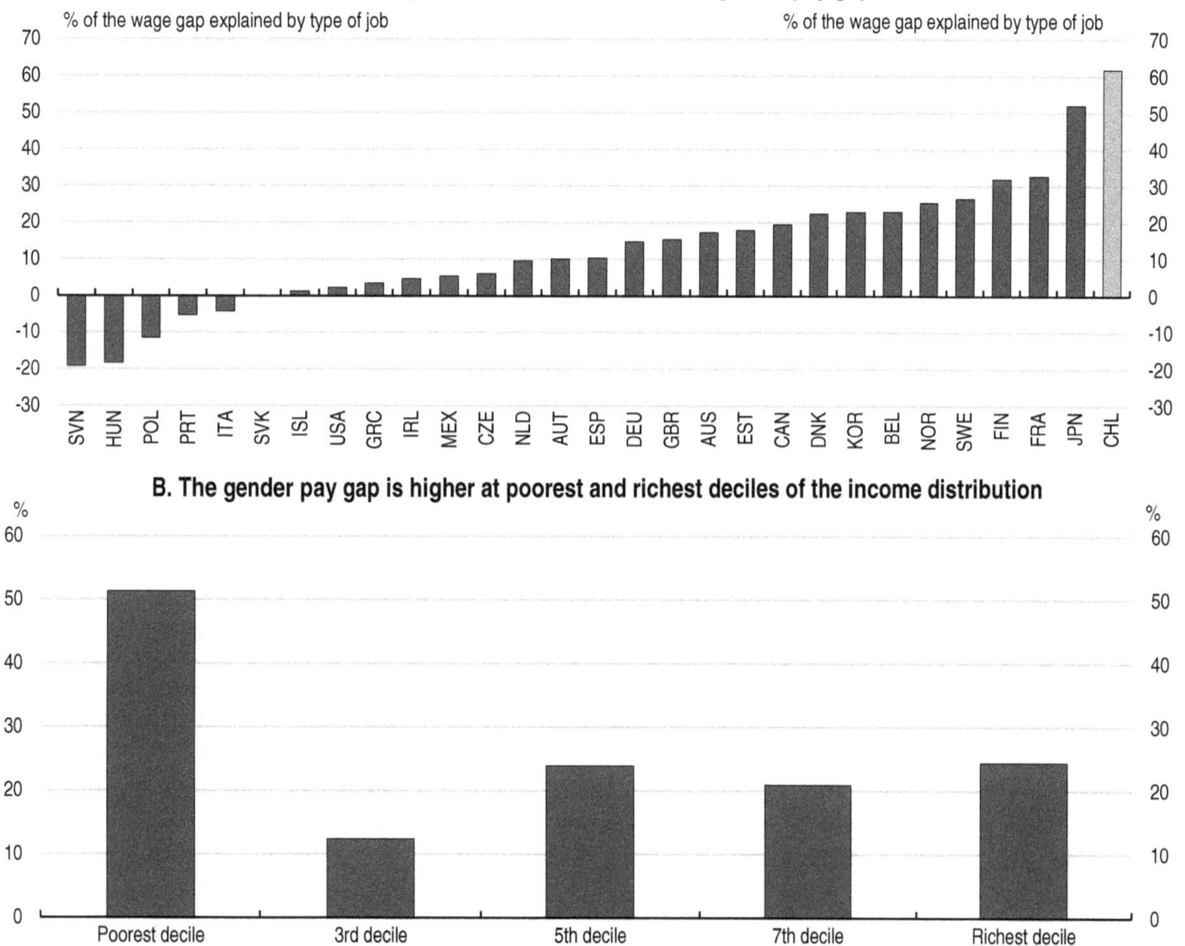

Source: For Chile OECD estimates based on CASEN (2013); for other countries OECD (2012b).

StatLink http://dx.doi.org/10.1787/888933302461

In addition, the gender pay gap varies a lot across the income distribution: it is higher at the extremes of the income distribution, in particular at the very bottom (Figure 1.13, Panel B). At lowest income levels, the job characteristics that depress women wages are firm size, informality and non-standard contracts. At highest income levels, the gender pay gap is explained by differences in education, occupation, and type of industry. While the level of education – women tend to be better educated than men – and type of occupation tend to reduce the gender pay gap, the type of industry where they are employed is the main factor contributing to increase it. This is probably related with a mismatch between girls' aspirations and their actual career achievements. Well-educated women often end up in jobs where they do not use their full potential and skills. In addition to loss of talent, OECD findings show that being over-qualified and over-skilled reduces job satisfaction, which is likely to reduce productivity (OECD, 2012b). To solve this problem, Chile should provide career guidance at schools and universities to help women better match their acquired skills with the career path they choose.

Reduce gender gaps to boost inclusive growth

Increasing participation of women in the labour force can have a significant impact on economic growth and contribute to reduce income inequality (OECD, 2012). First, research shows that Chile suffers one of the largest losses of income per capita because of low level of female labour force participation in the OECD (Figure 1.14, Panel A). Narrowing the labour force participation gap between men and women by 50% has been estimated to raise annual growth in GDP per capita by 0.3 percentage points on average (Thévenon et al., 2012). Second, Evidence from OECD countries shows that having more women in paid (full-time) work results in lower household income inequality (OECD, 2015b). Therefore, policies that focus on increasing the earnings potential of lower-paid women can reinforce the equalising effect of women's labour market integration.

Moreover, there appears to be a negative relationship between representation of women in parliaments and income inequality in OECD countries (Figure 1.15). Despite the fact that Chile has made remarkable progress increasing women participation in politics, the share of parliamentary seats occupied by women is the lowest in the OECD. Women's civic and political participation helps to promote their own rights as well as those of their families and communities. Women's civic activism pushes governments to be more responsive to women's claims and adopt gender-responsive policies. These policies must take into account the existence of discriminatory social institutions that can restrict women's ability to actively participate in public life. In some countries this includes limits on women's freedom of movement and negative attitudes towards female involvement in public life.

The government is making a strong effort to promote more gender diversity in leadership positions, both in parliament and in the boards of private companies. A new bill *Proyecto sobre fortalecimiento de la democracia*, contains provisions that seek to promote the political participation of women, giving funds to parties with the requirement that at least 10% of these funds are intended to encourage participation of women. Another bill, *Proyecto de ley sobre partidos políticos*, introduces quotas for women. It provides that for internal party elections candidates must respect gender balance where no sex should be represented in more than 60%. It also proposes mandatory participation of women in party relevant directives in order to achieve gender parity. Finally, as mentioned before, the labour reform currently being discussed in the Senate, makes mandatory the incorporation of women in the bargaining commissions for bargaining collectively, and requires firms to provide information about gender gaps in wages.

Enhance policies to help women join the labour force

Evidence shows that female labour supply is much more responsive to wage changes than males in terms of hours worked but even more so in terms of decision to participate (Killingsworth and Heckman, 1986). Because of this, active labour market policies that help improve skills and promote labour opportunities have a larger effect for women than for

Figure 1.14. **Gender gaps in the workforce contribute to income loss and high inequality**

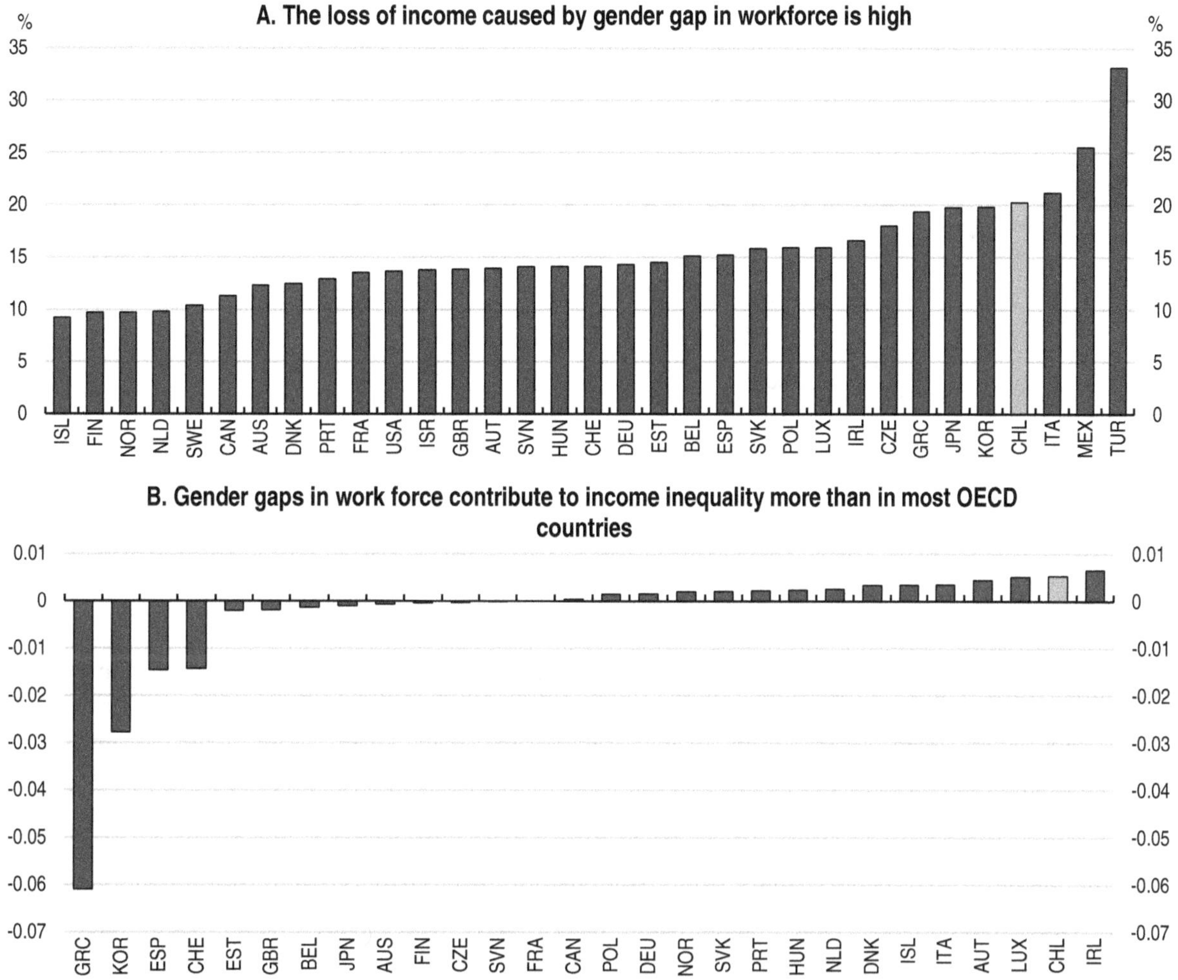

Note: In Panel B a negative (positive) contribution of a factor means a lower (higher) dispersion of that factor in the country considered relative to the United States, so that the factor drives inequality down (up) relative to the United States. The decomposition is based on the UQR results. To better capture the contribution of hours worked, a set of dummies is created, with each dummy capturing a bracket of five hours (Sweden is an exception since the dataset of that country only distinguishes between full-time and part-time workers).The results of the decomposition analysis need to be interpreted with care due to cross-country differences in survey designs and very small samples for several countries, most notably Iceland, Ireland, Luxembourg and Portugal.

Source: Panel A: Cuberes and Teignier (2015). Panel B: Fournier and Koske (2012).

StatLink http://dx.doi.org/10.1787/888933302472

men (Bergemann and Van den Berg, 2008). Since Chile devotes little public spending to active labour-market policies by international standards, more spending on this area can contribute to reduce the gender gap in labour force participation. Programmes like *MásCapaz* are a step in the right direction. This should be accompanied by steps to reduce the opportunity cost of joining the labour force, such as family benefits and child-related entitlements. Therefore, a key priority should be to expand high-quality childcare, especially for children aged up to three years. To help solve this problem, the government is building new child care spaces. The plan is to build more than 3 000 of these spaces during the period 2014-18.

Figure 1.15. **The number of women in parliament is correlated with income inequality**

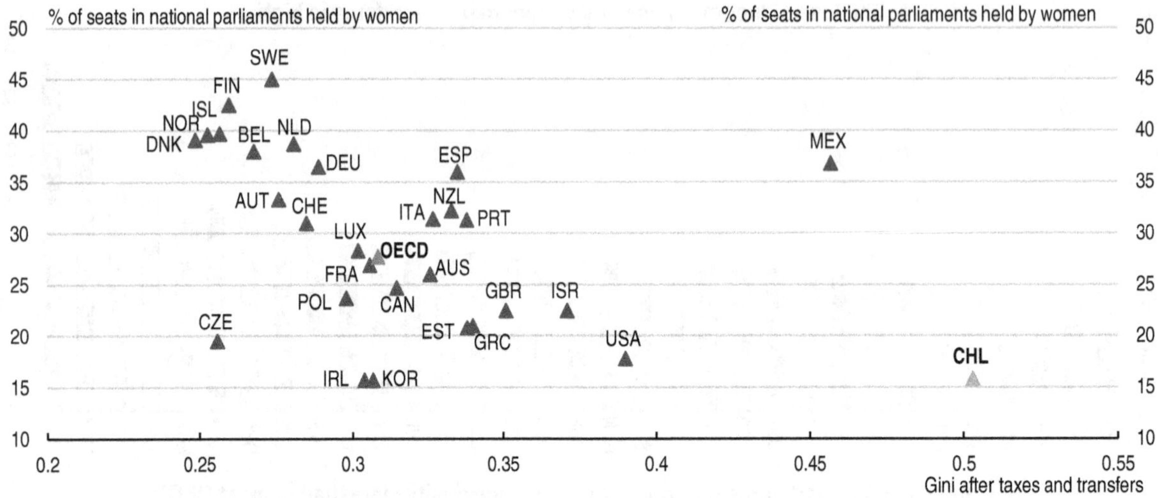

Source: *OECD Income Distribution and Poverty Database* and *PARLINE Database*.

StatLink http://dx.doi.org/10.1787/888933302486

Create awareness to fight discrimination

OECD evidence shows that an important part of the earnings gap between men and women is due to discrimination (Koske et al., 2012). Discrimination is likely to entail negative consequences for long-run living standards as it reduces work incentives and leads to a suboptimal allocation of human capital. To combat discrimination, legal rules can be made more effective, for example by empowering well-resourced specialised bodies to investigate employers even in the absence of individual complaints and to take legal action against those who engage in discriminatory practices (OECD, 2011). The fact that the Superintendence of Securities and Exchanges (*Superintendencia de Valores y Seguros*) is asking open stock companies to inform gender wage gaps in their annual reports, is a step in the right direction.

Policies to modify gender roles could also contribute to higher female labour market participation. Raising awareness for the existence of gender inequalities and for the potential benefits of a more gender-equal society is a prerequisite for broad support for a gender mainstreaming policy agenda. The newly created Ministry of Women is set to play a central role in bringing gender issues to the public debate through information campaigns or disseminating best practices can contribute to dismantling stereotypes such as the belief that a working mother is a bad mother or that technical professions are male professions.

Recommendations to bring all Chileans on board

A more inclusive labour market

- Reduce duality in the labour market between protected indefinite contracts and precarious fixed-term contracts.
- Strengthen public employment services to deliver targeted active labour market programmes for youth, the low-skilled and the unemployed.
- Increase spending in active labour market policies.

Improving the transfer system

- Increase mandatory pension contribution rates.
- Equalise the retirement age of men and women at 65 years.
- Link the retirement age according to changes in life expectancy.
- Boost the level of the solidarity pension.
- Enhance fiscal equalisation to ensure that poor municipalities have sufficient resources to provide their citizens with high quality services and continue efforts to improve these.
- Strengthen poverty alleviation policies as planned, better targeting them to vulnerable populations, including indigenous groups.

Closing gender gaps

- Improve the access to quality child-care for children under-3 years of age.
- Promote gender diversity in leadership positions in parliament and private companies.
- Bring gender issues into the public debate through information campaigns.

Bibliography

Barnay, T. (2014), "Health, Work and Working Conditions: A Review of the European Economic Literature", *TEPP Working Paper*, No. TEPP 2014-08, TEPP.

Bergemann, A. and G.J. van den Berg (2008), "Active Labor Market Policy Effects for Women in Europe – A Survey", *Annales d'Économie et de Statistique*, No. 91/92, pp. 385-408.

Bosio, G. (2014), "The Implications of Temporary Jobs on the Distribution of Wages in Italy: An Unconditional IVQTE Approach", *Labour*, Vol. 28, No. 1, pp. 64-86, March.

Bravo, D. et al. (2015), Presidential Advisory Commission on the Chilean Pension System, Santiago, *www.comision-pensiones.cl*.

Cahuc, P., O. Charlot and F. Malherbet (2012), "Explaining the Spread of Temporary Jobs and its Impact on Labor Turnover", *IZA Discussion Paper*, No. 6365, Bonn.

Causa, O. and Å. Johansson (2010), "Intergenerational Social Mobility in European OECD Countries", *OECD Journal: Economic Studies*, Vol. 2010.

Chen, W.H. et al. (2015), "Nonstandard Work and Inequality", *OECD Social, Employment and Migration Working Papers*, OECD, Paris.

Cingano, F. (2014), "Trends in Income Inequality and its Impact on Economic Growth", *OECD Social, Employment and Migration Working Papers*, No. 163.

Corak, M. (2013), "Inequality from Generation to Generation: The United States in Comparison", in R. Rycroft (ed.), *The Economics of Inequality, Poverty, and Discrimination in the 21st Century*, Santa Barbara, CA: ABC-CLIO.

Diaz Vidal, D. (2014), "Chile: Mobility among the Oligarchs", in Gregoy Clark, *The Son Also Rises: Surnames and the History of Social Mobility*, Princeton University Press.

Engel, E., A. Galetovic and C. Raddatz (1999), "Taxes and income distribution in Chile: some unpleasant redistributive arithmetic", *Journal of Development Economics*, Vol. 59, pp. 155-192.

Fairfield, T. and M. Jorratt (2015), "Top income shares, business profits, and effective tax rates in contemporary Chile", *Review of Income and Wealth*, forthcoming.

Fournier, J.M. and I. Koske (2012), "Less Income Inequality and More Growth – Are They Compatible? Part 7. The Drivers of Labour Earnings Inequality – An Analysis Based on Conditional and Unconditional Quantile Regressions", *OECD Economics Department Working Papers*, No. 930.

Fredriksen, K. (2012), "Less Income Inequality and More Growth – Are They Compatible? Part 6. The Distribution of Wealth", *OECD Economics Department Working Paper*, No. 929.

Freeman, R. et al. (2015), "Bargaining for the American Dream: What Unions do for Mobility", *www.americanprogress.org*.

Gauthier, A.H., T.M. Smeedeng and F.F. Furstenberg (2014) "Are Parents Investing Less Time in Children? Trends in Selected Industrialized Countries", *Population and Development Review*, Vol. 30(4).

Hoeller, P. et al. (2012), "Less Income Inequality and More Growth – Are They Compatible? Part 1. Mapping Income Inequality across the OECD", *OECD Economics Department Working Papers*, No. 924.

Horvath, R. (2012), "Does Trust Promote Growth?", *IOS Working Papers*, No. 319, July 2012.

Joumard, I., M. Pisu and D. Bloch (2012), "Less Income Inequality and More Growth – Are They Compatible? Part 3. Income Redistribution via Taxes and Transfers across OECD Countries", *OECD Economics Department Working Papers*, No. 926.

Kierzenkowski, R. and I. Koske (2012), "Less Income Inequality and More Growth – Are They Compatible? Part 8. The Drivers of Labour Income Inequality – A Review of the Recent Literature", *OECD Economics Department Working Papers*, No. 931.

Killingsworth, M. and J. Heckman (1986), "Labor supply of women", in Ashenfelter and Layard (eds.), *Handbook of Labor Economics*, Vol. 1.

Koske, I., J.M. Fournier and I. Wanner (2012), "Less Income Inequality and More Growth – Are They Compatible? Part 2. The Distribution of Labour Income", *OECD Economics Department Working Papers*, No. 925.

Larrañaga, O. et al. (2014), "Presente y futuro de la política de capacitación en Chile", *Documentos de Trabajo Área de Reducción de la Pobreza y la Desigualdad*, PNUD.

López, R., E. Figueroa and P. Gutiérrez (2013), "La 'parte del león': Nuevas estimaciones de la participación de los súper ricos en el ingreso de Chile", *Serie de Documentos de Trabajo*, No. 379.

López, R., E. Figueroa and P. Gutiérrez (2015), "Fundamental accrued capital gains and the measurement of top incomes: An application to Chile", *Serie de Documentos de Trabajo*, No. 409.

Lopez, R. and S. Miller (2008), "Chile: The Unbearable Burden of Inequality", *World Development*, Vol. 36, No. 12, pp. 2679-2695.

Lustig, N. (2015), "Inequality and Fiscal Redistribution in Middle Income Countries: Brazil, Chile, Colombia, Indonesia, Mexico, Peru and South Africa", *Center for Global Development Working Papers*, No. 410, August.

Núnez, J. and R. Gutiérrez (2004), "Class discrimination and meritocracy in the labor market: evidence from Chile", *Estudios de Economía*, Vol. 31, Department of Economics, University of Chile, pp. 113-132, December.

Núñez, J. and L. Miranda (2011), "Intergenerational income and educational mobility in urban Chile", *Estudios de Economía*, Vol. 38, No. 1, pp. 195-221, June.

OECD (2006), *Boosting Jobs and Incomes – Policy Lessons from Reassessing the OECD Jobs Strategy*, OECD, Paris.

OECD (2010), *OECD Employment Outlook 2010: Moving Beyond the Jobs Crisis*, OECD Publishing, Paris.

OECD (2011a), *Divided We Stand: Why Inequality Keeps Rising*, OECD Publishing, Paris.

OECD (2011b), *Doing Better for Families*, OECD Publishing, Paris.

OECD (2012a), "Income Inequality and Growth: The Role of Taxes and Transfers", *OECD Economics Department Policy Note*, No. 9.

OECD (2012b), *Closing the Gender Gap: Act Now*, OECD Publishing, Paris.

OECD (2014), *Education at a Glance 2014: OECD Indicators*, OECD Publishing, Paris.

OECD (2015a), *In it Together: Why Less Inequality Benefits All*, OECD Publishing, Paris.

OECD (2015b), *All on Board: Making Inclusive Growth Happen*, OECD Publishing, Paris.

OECD (2015c), *Chile: Policies Priorities for Stronger and more Equitable Growth*, OECD, Paris.

OECD (2015d), *OECD Skills Outlook 2015: Youth, Skills and Employability*, OECD Publishing, Paris.

Ostry, J.D., A. Berg and C.G. Tsangarides (2014), "Redistribution, Inequality, and Growth", *IMF Staff Discussion Note*, No. SDN/14/02.

Rau, T. (2011). "Pobreza y desigualdad en Chile: Un análisis con la Encuesta Casen", pp. 163-201, in G. Reinecke and M.E. Valenzuela (eds.), *El impacto del mercado laboral en el bienestar de las personas*, OIT, Santiago, Chile.

Reinecke, G. and M.E. Valenzuela (2011). "Distribución y mercado de trabajo: Un vínculo ineludible", pp. 163-201, in G. Reinecke and M.E. Valenzuela (eds.), *El impacto del mercado laboral en el bienestar de las personas*, OIT, Santiago, Chile.

Santangelo, G. (2011), "Do Temporary Contracts Cause Wage Discrimination? A Quantile Treatment Effect Analysis for Europe", mimeo.

Sunkel, O. and R. Infante (2009), "Hacia un desarrollo inclusivo: el caso de Chile", CEPAL, Fundación Chile 21, OIT, Santiago, Chile.

Thévenon, O. et al. (2012), "Effects of Reducing Gender Gaps in Education and Labour Force Participation on Economic Growth in the OECD", *OECD Social, Employment and Migration Working Papers*, No. 138, OECD Publishing, Paris.

Torche, F. (2005), "Unequal but fluid: social mobility in Chile in comparative perspective", *American Sociological Review*, Vol. 70(3), pp. 422-450.

Uslaner, E. and M. Brown (2005), "Inequality, Trust, and Civic Engagement", *American Politics Research*, Vol. 33, pp. 868-894.

Venn, D. (2009), "Legislation, collective bargaining and enforcement: Updating the OECD employment protection indicators", *OECD Employment Affairs Working Papers*.

World Bank (2015), "Efectos Distributivos de la Reforma Tributaria de 2014", *World Bank Document*, Latin America and Carribean.

Chapter 2

Better skills for inclusive growth

Improving education and skills is the linchpin to reduce income inequality and boost productivity growth. This chapter argues that to improve, and make better use of, the skills of the labour force, Chile could gain a lot from a comprehensive and consistent Skills Strategy along three pillars: developing, activating and using skills effectively. Chile has made tremendous progress over the last decades attracting more students to the education system. Yet, educational outcomes remain below OECD standards, and are strongly linked to students' socio-economic status. Improving the quality and equity of education would help achieve stronger productivity growth and make Chile a more inclusive country. Therefore, Chile should set the goal of attaining universal skills by 2030. Reaching this goal requires investing more in early childhood education, making schools more inclusive and reshaping teacher careers. Chile also needs to improve access to quality tertiary education for students from medium and low socio-economic backgrounds. Finally, in terms of activating and using skills effectively, a key goal should be to reduce skill mismatch, which contributes to low productivity growth. This requires more flexible labour markets, investing more in vocational education and training, and promoting the participation of more women in the fields of engineering and computer science.

Education and skills development can play a key role in reducing income inequality and increasing productivity, both of which are constraining growth in Chile. Developing better skills is critical in the structural adjustment of economies, and can help the Chilean economy rebalance and move from a relative dependence on commodities production to high value added manufacturing and service industries. Inability to learn new skills because of inadequate basic education or lack of opportunity will slow the transfer of all factors of production from lower to higher value added activities. Furthermore, education and skills also have a vital role to play in improving equalities of opportunity (Chapter 1), which requires that access to quality education be equal, especially during early childhood. Enhancing the quality of education for all will also improve people's lives, as educated individuals live longer, participate more actively in politics and in the community where they live, commit fewer crimes and rely less on social assistance (OECD, 2013a).

This chapter argues that to improve, and make better use of, the skills of the labour force, Chile needs a comprehensive and consistent Skills Strategy. This requires actions along three pillars: developing, activating and using skills effectively. In terms of developing skills, Chile still has a lot to do to catch up with OECD standards (Brandt, 2010). The performance gap with respect to the OECD average is the equivalent of 1.7 years of secondary schooling, with large differences based on gender and socio-economic status. Therefore, Chile should set the goal of reaching universal basic skills by 2030 – a level that, when fully attained, is assumed to represent the basic skills necessary for participating productively in modern economies. Setting a quantitative goal is crucial, as improvement in education is not possible if policies are not related to clear objectives framed in terms of learning outcomes (OECD, 2015d). To reach this goal, Chile's government has taken important measures to invest more in early childhood education and care, make schools more inclusive and reshape teacher careers. It is also promoting policies to improve access to quality tertiary education for students from medium and low socio-economic backgrounds.

Then, in terms of activating skills, better policies to facilitate the transition from school to work are necessary, as 22% of 15-29 year-olds were neither employed nor in education or training in 2011 (OECD, 2015g). In this regard, more investment in vocational education and training, both at upper-secondary and postsecondary level, can help students better prepare for the labour market. Finally, in terms of using skills effectively, Chile, like many other countries, usually struggles with low productivity levels and skills mismatches among the labour force. Therefore, it would benefit from skills policies being better aligned with overall economic goals. This requires complementing strong education with more flexible labour market institutions, as this is crucial to allocate skills efficiently to boost productivity in an inclusive manner.

Skills, productivity and inclusive growth

Despite the large improvements of the last three decades, income gaps between Chile and other OECD countries remain large, and about 80% of this gap is explained by differences in labour productivity (Figure 2.1). To close the income gap Chile needs to boost

Figure 2.1. **Chile needs to increase labour productivity to catch up with best performing OECD countries**

A. Differences in GDP per capita relative to the upper half of OECD countries

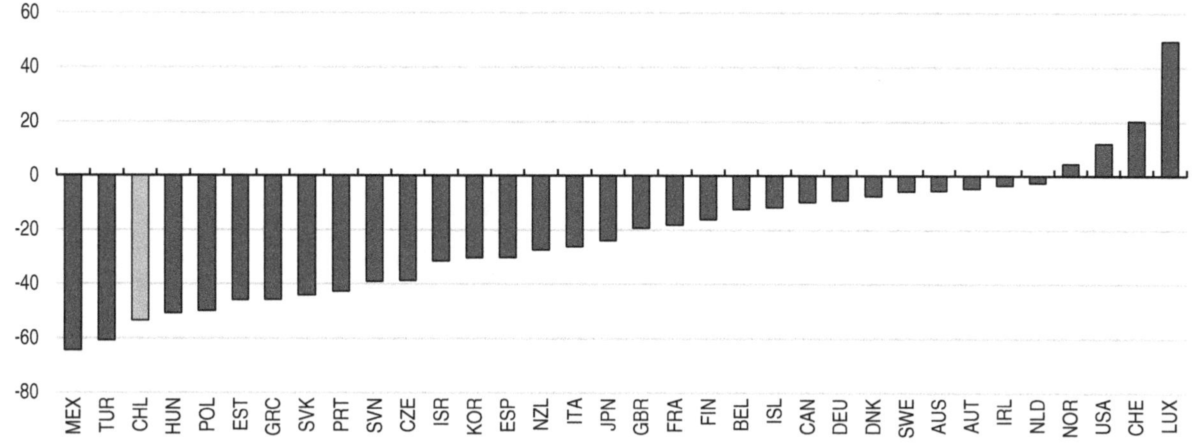

B. Differences in GDP per capita explained by differences in labour productivity

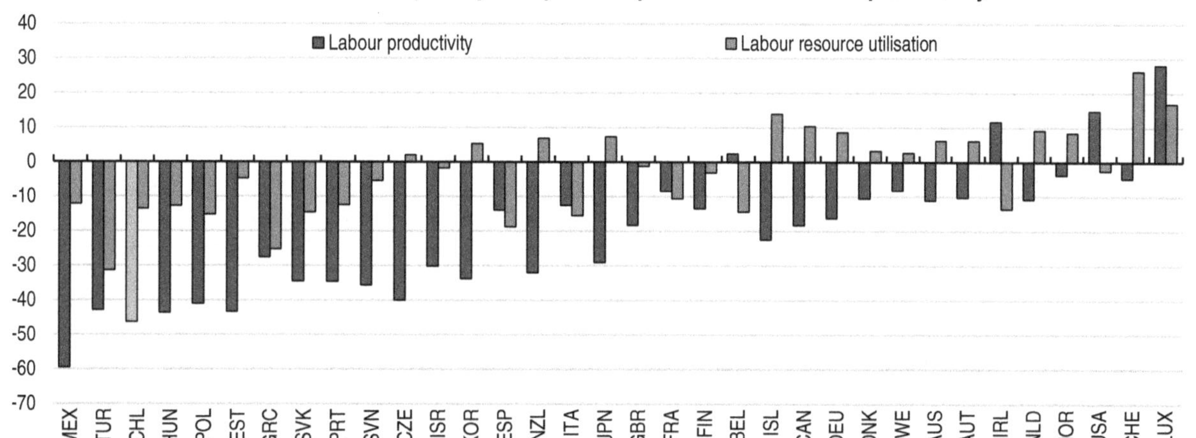

Source: OECD (2015b), *Economic Policy Reforms 2015: Going for Growth.*

StatLink http://dx.doi.org/10.1787/888933302496

labour productivity which is necessary to create quality jobs and improve well-being. This requires increasing the quality of human capital by improving the skills of the labour force. There is a large body of evidence showing the importance of skills in determining the productivity of individuals, and the value of education in raising skills (Heckman and Masterov, 2007). Skills are as important in combating poverty and exclusion as they are in maintaining competitiveness and employability (ILO, 2007). Education, training, and lifelong learning foster a virtuous circle of higher productivity and more employment, which improves the quality of life and boosts income growth. Inequalities in educational attainment and skills can have an adverse impact on overall productivity in times of rapid technological change (Goldin and Katz, 2007).

The Chilean educational system has grown rapidly and today nearly all children between the ages of 5 and 17 are in school (OECD, 2014a). Currently, the share of the population with at least upper secondary education is above the OECD average for younger adults (Figure 2.2). However, increasing enrolment rates does not necessarily generate significant economic gains (Pritchett, 2006). In Chile, the economic benefits from enrolling

Figure 2.2. **Upper secondary education attainment is relatively high among young adults**

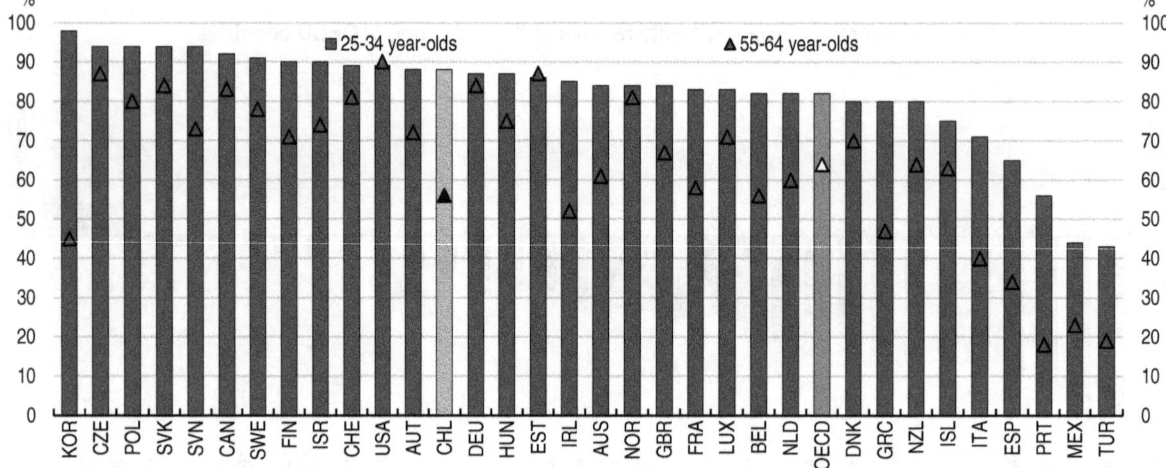

Source: OECD (2014a), *Education at a Glance 2014: OECD Indicators.*

StatLink http://dx.doi.org/10.1787/888933302501

all children have been limited because the quality of education remains well below the OECD average, and there are profound inequalities across socio-economic groups (OECD, 2015e). The average student in Chile has a PISA score of 422 out of 600 in reading, maths and science, much lower than the OECD average of 497. And the average difference in results between the students with the highest socio-economic background and the students with the lowest socio-economic background is 105 points, significantly higher than the OECD average of 96 points. Chile also has the lowest share of students who beat the socio-economic odds against them and exceed expectations (Figure 2.3).

Figure 2.3. **A low share of students beat the socio-economic odds stacked against them**

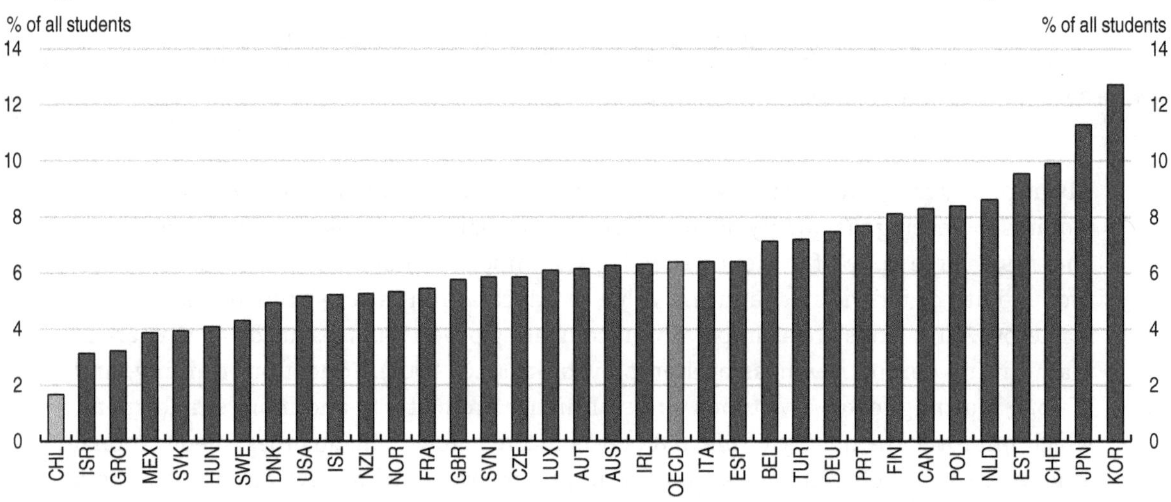

Note: A student is classified as resilient if he or she is in the bottom quarter of the PISA index of economic, social and cultural status (ESCS) in the country of assessment and performs in the top quarter of students among all countries, after accounting for socio-economic status. Countries and economies are ranked in ascending order of the percentage of resilient students.

Source: OECD, *PISA 2012 Database.*

StatLink http://dx.doi.org/10.1787/888933302512

Attaining universal skills to boost economic growth

The first step to improve the skills of the labour force in the long run is to ensure that all young people leave school with a range of basic and relevant skills. In Chile a significant proportion of young people are unable to demonstrate full attainment of Level 1 of skills in PISA exams (Figure 2.4, Panel A). This level of skills (420 points on the PISA mathematics scale), when fully attained, is assumed to represent the basic skills necessary for participating productively in modern economies. A level at which students can answer questions involving familiar contexts where all relevant information is present and the questions are clearly defined. Having a large share of the population below this skill level presents a big obstacle for productivity growth in Chile.

Figure 2.4. **Improving the quality of education can boost GDP growth**

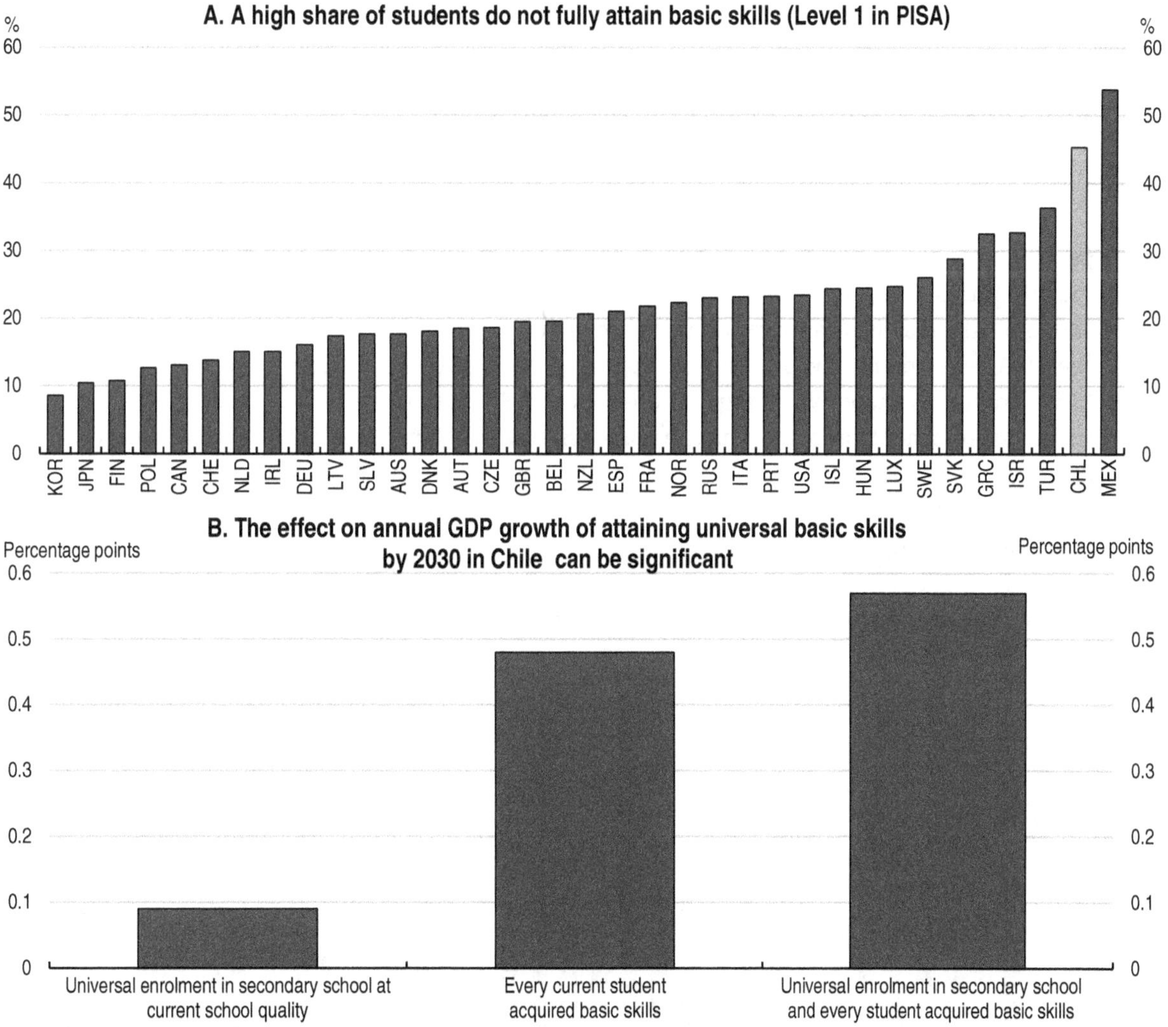

A. A high share of students do not fully attain basic skills (Level 1 in PISA)

%
60
50
40
30
20
10
0
KOR JPN FIN POL CAN CHE NLD IRL DEU LTV SLV AUS DNK AUT CZE GBR BEL NZL ESP FRA NOR RUS ITA PRT USA ISL HUN LUX SWE SVK GRC ISR TUR CHL MEX

B. The effect on annual GDP growth of attaining universal basic skills by 2030 in Chile can be significant

Percentage points
0.6
0.5
0.4
0.3
0.2
0.1
0
Universal enrolment in secondary school at current school quality
Every current student acquired basic skills
Universal enrolment in secondary school and every student acquired basic skills

Note: Panel B: The bars refer to increase in annual growth rate (in percentage points) once the whole labour force has reached the specific goal.
Source: OECD (2015d).

StatLink http://dx.doi.org/10.1787/888933302267

The potential gains of attaining universal skills – when all students fully attain Level 1 in PISA exams – can be very large. OECD estimates suggest that ensuring universal access to secondary education by 2030 at the current level of quality can only yield some economic gains increasing Chile's annual economic growth by 0.09 percentage points and real GDP will be 1.3% higher by 2030 (Figure 2.4, Panel B). However, improving quality of schools so that each of the current students attains basic skills by 2030 – assuming that all students who score above 420 PISA points remain at their current level – can have a much stronger impact on the economy. In particular, Chile's annual economic growth can increase by 0.48 percentage points per year or an increase of 7% in real GDP by 2030. Furthermore, if the two previous scenarios are combined and Chile ensures universal access to secondary education and full attainment of basic skills of all students by 2030, the increase in the annual growth rate of GDP would be 0.57 percentage points, which means that real GDP will be 8.5% higher by 2030. Almost all of the gain comes from improving achievement at the bottom end, since enrolment in Chile is already very high. Therefore, the key for Chile is to focus on improving the quality of pre-primary, primary and secondary education to provide universal basic skills.

Developing universal skills through quality education

In Chile students' socio-economic background strongly influences educational performance, with the impact of socio-economic status on students' performance in mathematics being one of the largest in the OECD (Figure 2.5). While many socio-economically disadvantaged students succeed at school, and some achieve high levels on the PISA assessment, socio-economic status is still a strong predictor of performance in Chile, and is associated with large differences in PISA. Furthermore, a large percentage of the between-school variance in performance is explained by the schools' socio-economic background (OECD, 2015e). Socio-economically advantaged students and schools tend to outscore their disadvantaged peers by larger margins than between any other two groups of students (OECD, 2015e).

Figure 2.5. **Socio-economically advantaged students outscored their disadvantaged peers**

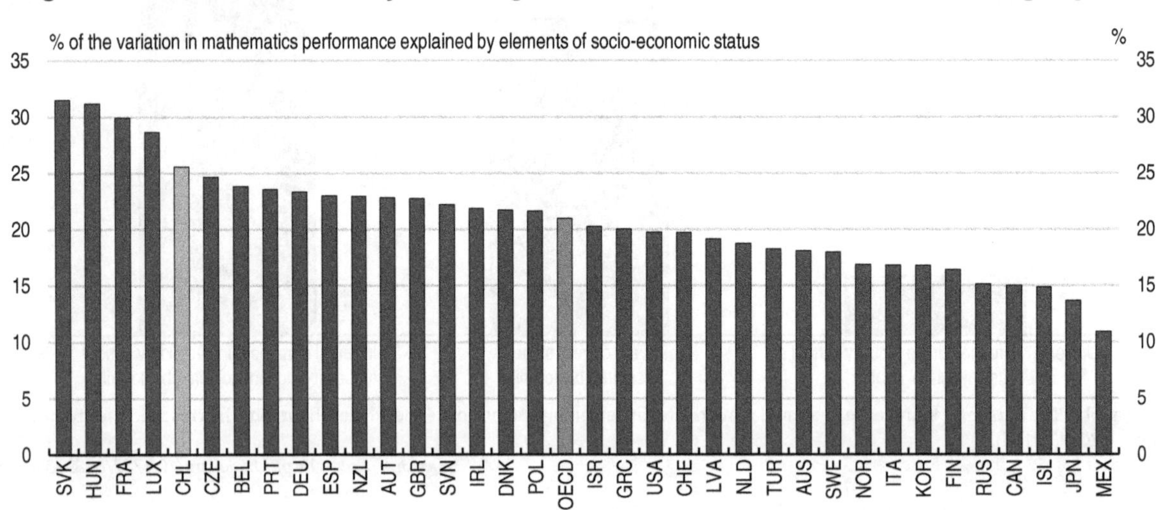

Source: PISA participants, based on PISA 2012 micro data.

StatLink http://dx.doi.org/10.1787/888933302520

Invest more in early childhood education

More investment in early childhood education can help reduce the gap generated by family environments early in life. Empirical evidence shows that early childhood care support can help reduce high school dropout rates, improve student performance and reduce gaps in learning achievement generated by different social backgrounds (Heckman, 2013; OECD, 2011). Early learning confers value on acquired skills, which leads to self-reinforcing motivation to learn more. Early mastery of a range of cognitive, social, and emotional competencies makes learning at later ages more efficient and therefore easier and more likely to continue.

Early childhood education is particularly relevant for children from disadvantaged environments who typically do not receive the same degree of early enrichment that children from middle-income and upper-income families receive. Evidence using data from Chile's Early Childhood Longitudinal Survey show that the differences in early childhood development emerge early, and that there is a marked correlation between family income, maternal education, cognitive and non-cognitive development, and the health of children (Contreras et al., 2015). These highlight the need to increase efforts to expand the coverage of childcare and early childhood high quality education services.

In Chile, the coverage limitations at this level are due to the inadequate supply of services and the high costs that would be involved if families had to pay for these services in the private sector, particularly families in medium and low-income sectors. Despite recent advances, enrolment in childcare is still low compared with other OECD countries. For children between 0 and 24 months, Chile has one of the lowest coverage (11% compared with 29% in the OECD average). For children aged 25-48 months, the coverage level of 43% is clearly low when compared with the OECD average of 70%. In the group of five year old, fully universal coverage has still not been achieved even though this level has been mandatory since 2013.

Annual spending per child in pre-primary education puts Chile in 24th place among the 36 countries of the OECD. Current coverage of early childhood education services also shows differences based on families' socio-economic levels. Children between the ages of 49 and 72 months and between the ages of 25 and 48 months show coverage gaps between the richest and poorest quintiles of nearly 10% and 15%, respectively. For children aged 0 to 24 months the coverage percentages are similar across income quintiles (Figure 2.6, Panel A), but with levels that are still very low in comparison with potential demand and the rates observed in other OECD countries (Figure 2.6, Panel B). This situation is concerning because the most vulnerable households are those that make the least use of childcare and early childhood education services, particularly for children between 0 and 4 years of age, when it is in those households that early childhood education interventions can have the greatest impact.

The government has established the goal of expanding early childhood education. A new programme aims to increase the coverage of preschool education throughout Chile, and to improve and monitor quality through the creation the Secretariat for Childhood Education and the Superintendent of Preschool Education (*Subsecretaría de Educación Parvularia y la Intendencia de Educación Parvularia*). The current administration also plans to create 534 new nurseries in a first stage. This will enable more than ten thousand children between zero and two years to have access to early childcare and education. Furthermore, in the next four years it hopes to create new spaces for daycare and new spaces in the middle level of nursery school, which would bring Chile close to average coverage levels in the OECD.

Figure 2.6. **Coverage of childcare and pre-school services is low across all income quintiles**

A. Participation rates for 0-3 year olds in formal childcare and pre-school services across income groups

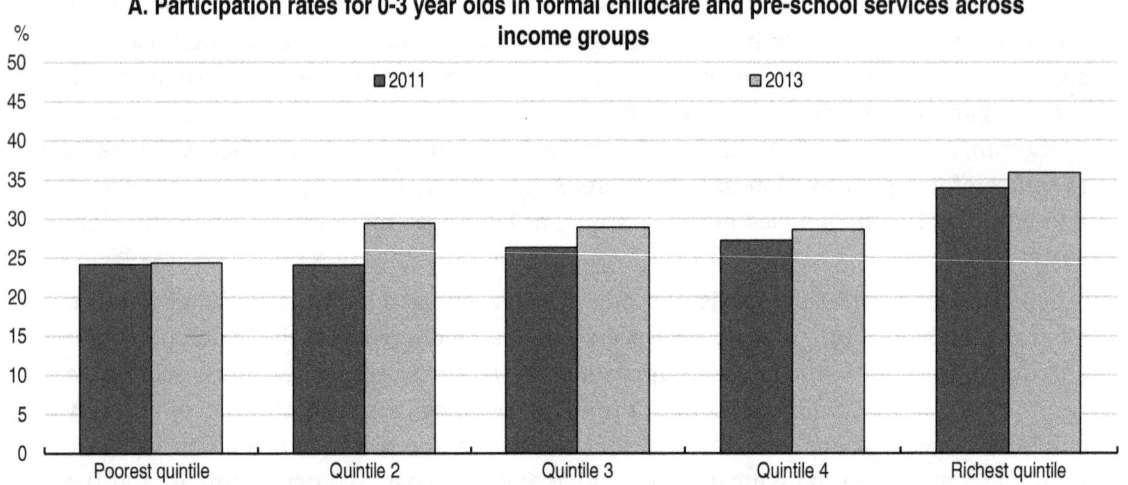

B. Participation rates for 0-2 year olds in formal childcare and pre-school services in OECD countries

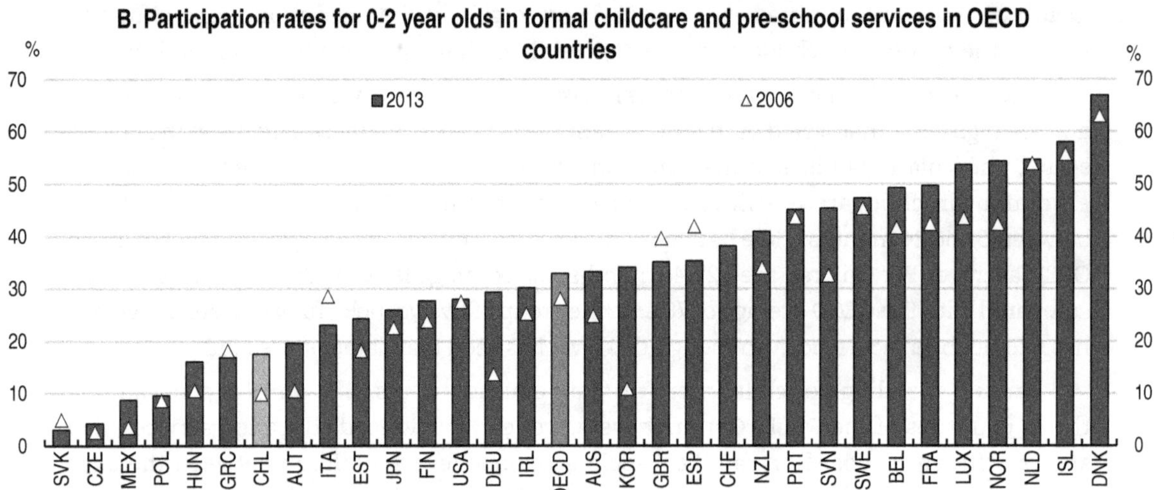

Source: Panel A: CASEN (2011 and 2013). Panel B: OECD, *Family Database*.

StatLink http://dx.doi.org/10.1787/888933302536

Build more inclusive schools

Chile introduced in 1981 nationwide school choice by providing vouchers to any student wishing to attend private school. As a result, more than 1 000 private schools entered the market, and the private enrolment rate increased by 20 percentage points, with greater impacts in wealthier communities. Evidence shows that this policy led to increased sorting between students and schools without significant improvements in terms of quality (Hsieh and Urquiola, 2006). The reason is that some of the intended benefits of competition are not necessarily related to student achievement, while there are potential disadvantages in terms of equity and social inclusion. There are large differences across neighbourhoods (Figure 2.7): those with lower income per capita and higher inequality rates have lower quality of education as measured by the *Sistema de Medición de Calidad de la Educación* (SIMCE) exams results.

Figure 2.7. **Quality of education varies a lot by municipality and region, and is correlated with income**

A. Quality of education is highly correlated with income in Santiago area

B. The quality of education varies by province

C. Quality of education is correlated with income per capita

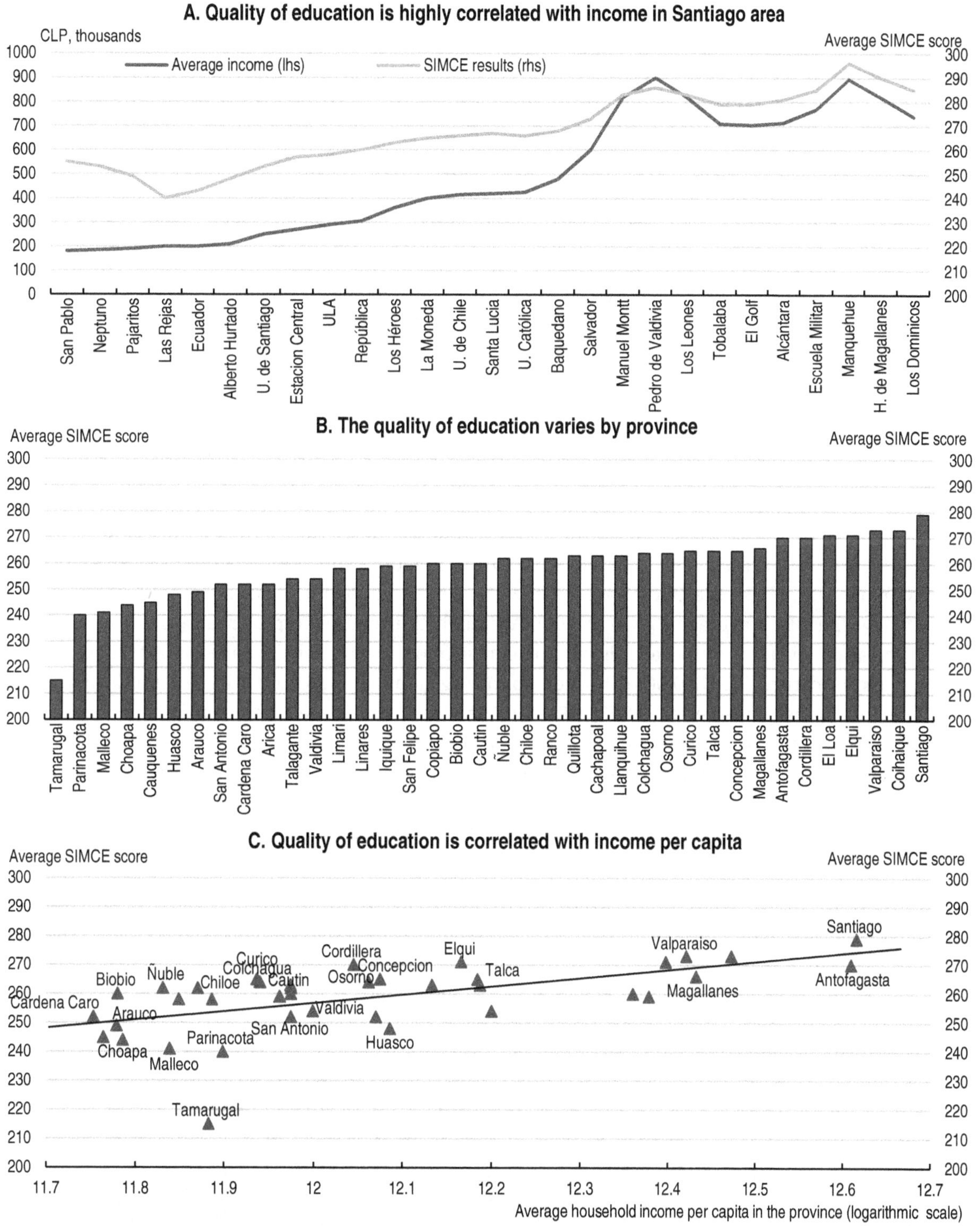

Source: CASEN (2013) and SIMCE (2011).

StatLink http://dx.doi.org/10.1787/888933302545

Student selection exacerbates differences between students in part because less demanding schools tend to provide less stimulating learning environments, but also because students' outcomes are affected by peers (Field, Kuczera and Pont, 2007). Students from lower socio-economic background are particularly affected by academic selection because they are disproportionally placed in lower quality schools, widening initial inequities (Spinath and Spinath, 2005). When schools are allowed to select students based on their ability, competition leads to stratification by parental income, increasing transmission of income inequality, and reducing student effort (MacLeod and Urquiola, 2009). On the contrary, when schools cannot select students based upon their ability, strong competition between them is efficient, encouraging entry by high productivity schools and increasing the average skill levels of students (MacLeod and Urquiola, 2009).

To eliminate practices that hinder equity and target low-performing disadvantaged schools and students, the current administration has taken important steps. Earlier this year Congress passed the Inclusion and Equity Law, which aims to eliminate school selection, the elimination of for-profit schools, and the elimination of co-payments in all schools receiving public funds. Improving the quality of public schools is necessary to attract more students from high socio-economic backgrounds. This can help improve the social mix and increase social mobility. Evidence produced for this report shows that educational mobility in Chile is higher in regions with a stronger presence of public schools – where higher shares of students attend public schools (Box 1.1, Chapter 1).

Over the past decade, Chile has steadily expanded its education spending to 6.9% of GDP in 2011, above the OECD average of 6.1%. However, spending per students remains below the OECD average (OECD, 2014a). Although the relationship between the level of education spending and quality is not linear, research shows that below a certain threshold of expenditure (USD 50 000), higher spending is associated with better students' performance (Baket et al., 2002; OECD 2015e). As Chile is well below this threshold (Figure 2.8), increasing spending in education per student may help improve educational quality. Furthermore, evidence also shows that how resources are allocated across schools

Figure 2.8. **Average spending per student between the ages of 6 and 15 is low**

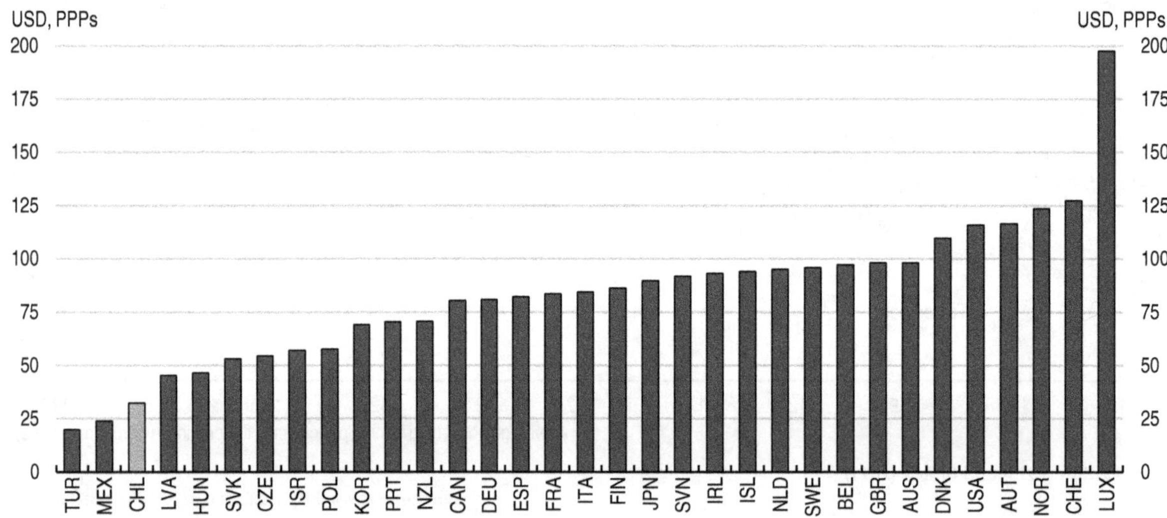

Note: Spending is measured in USD PPPs in the year 2012.
Source: OECD, *PISA 2012 Database*.

StatLink http://dx.doi.org/10.1787/888933302278

is also very important; in particular, how resources are allocated between disadvantaged and advantaged schools. A more equal distribution of resources (in terms of quality of physical infrastructure and schools' educational resources) is associated with better test results (OECD, 2015e).

Chile needs to develop a better methodology for funding schools so that it focuses on those that have the greatest needs. For this to happen, monitoring should be improved for both effectiveness and efficiency. In this regard, the implementation of the education superintendence (*Superintendencia de Educación*) has been a positive development. This institution is responsible for auditing and supervising compliance of school providers with relevant laws standards and regulation.

Reshape teacher careers

Chile has a shortage of qualified teachers (Figure 2.9), and thus needs to select and recruit the most effective trainee teachers, with training programmes that are selective and rigorous (OECD, 2010). Bringing the best into teaching requires recruiting from the top-third of each graduating cohort (Barber and Mourshed, 2007). Candidates should qualify for an all-graduate profession through a university-based programme that rigorously connects research with practical training (Schleicher, 2011). Currently, Chile does not use specific selective requirements other than diploma and grade-point average in secondary education to select candidates into teacher training and thus candidates have been found to obtain low scores on the university selection test *Prueba de Selección Universitaria* (PSU) (Santiago et al., 2013). After graduation, teachers need not meet either additional requirements to start teaching (such as passing competitive examinations or a standardised test), and have no registration or probation process once in practice. However, in the public sector (municipal schools) teachers have to pass a mandatory Teacher Evaluation (Evaluación Docente) every four years.

Figure 2.9. **The percentage of certified teachers reported by school principals in PISA is very low**

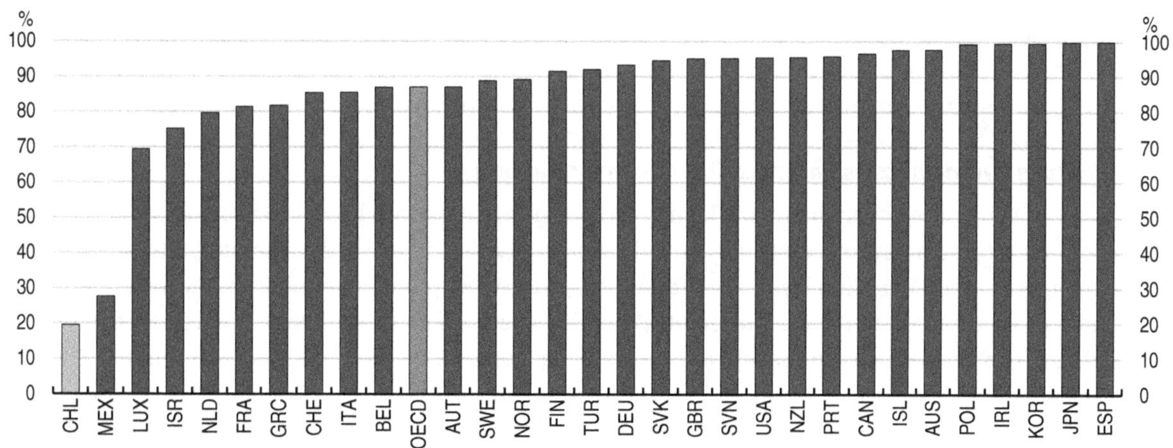

Source: OECD, *PISA 2012 Database.*

StatLink http://dx.doi.org/10.1787/888933302557

Universities can decide whether or not to provide teaching experience during initial teacher education. And graduating teachers thus tend to lack pedagogical knowledge (Santiago et al., 2013). Diversifying career growth possibilities is also important. Chile could define career steps in teacher development (e.g. beginning, classroom teacher, experienced teacher) to permit a better match between teacher competence and skills and the tasks performed at schools. Teaching conditions, such as salaries, workload and support received at schools also matter to motivate and help teachers improve. Chile should direct new resources into teaching in strategic ways. Compared to the OECD average, teachers in Chile have one of the highest numbers of teaching hours per year, lower salaries compared to those of other tertiary educated professions in the country, and work in schools with some of the largest disparities in the allocation of resources.

Chile has made important progress in standards of practice as well as in teacher appraisal, but challenges remain. Currently, a bill to reform teachers' career is in Congress (*Plan Nacional Docente*). The bill makes the teacher career more selective, raising the requirements to enter them. It increases demands on educational institutions, so as to ensure that graduates have the knowledge and skills that are required. It also increases significantly the compensation at the beginning of the profession, even above the average of the salaries of other university graduates. It creates a staged career that recognises merit and experience more attractive to those who are at higher levels wage profiles, and improves the teacher evaluation system. Finally, it increases the proportion of non-lecturing hours, allowing teachers more time for lesson preparation, design and correction of assessments, care of students, collaborative work, etc.

Ensuring all adults can access quality higher education and get the right skills

To promote equity and increase productivity Chile must also ensure that high quality tertiary education system is accessible to students from the traditionally excluded groups and that bright children from poor families are no longer less likely to graduate from university than much less able children from affluent families (Figure 2.10, Panel A). In recent decades Chile has made significant progress to reduce vertical inequality by expanding access to tertiary education to students from all income groups (Figure 2.10, Panels B and C). This high growth of enrolment rates has been driven mainly by the rapid expansion of the private sector, which accounts for about 75% of overall enrolment (Espinoza and Urzua, 2014). However, since the gap between enrolment among the top and bottom income quintiles remain large, efforts need to be enhanced to ensure that students from low socio-economic background can access high tertiary education institutions.

Reduce financial constraints to low income students

In Chile, the government works in partnership with private banks to provide student loans by offering an interest rate subsidy, and a guarantee in case of default. This has, however, resulted in high levels of student debt, while the quality of education received did not generate rates of return sufficient to service sustainably these debts, particularly for those from vulnerable families. To reduce financial constraints faced by these students, the government is considering providing free higher education in 2016 to all students from families that are below the 5th decile of the income distribution that enrol in higher education institutions that fulfil some quality and governance requirements. The government will present to Congress a bill to finance and regulate higher education. This policy will certainly help reduce financial constraints to access tertiary education for many students from lower income families, but may not necessarily be the best solution.

Figure 2.10. **Access to tertiary education has improved but remains unequal**

A. Educational mobility is low

%
100
90
80
70
60
50
40
30
20
10
0

No education
Primary education
Medium education (academic)
Medium education (technical / professional)
High technical (1-3 years)
Professional (4 years or more)
Postgraduate

Highest educational level of the parents

Own education level
- Postgraduate degree
- Professional degree (4 years or more)
- Higher technical degree (1-3 years)
- Medium education (technico-professional)
- Medium education (scientific & humanities)
- Primary education
- No education

B. Enrolment in tertiary education has increased faster than in the average OECD country

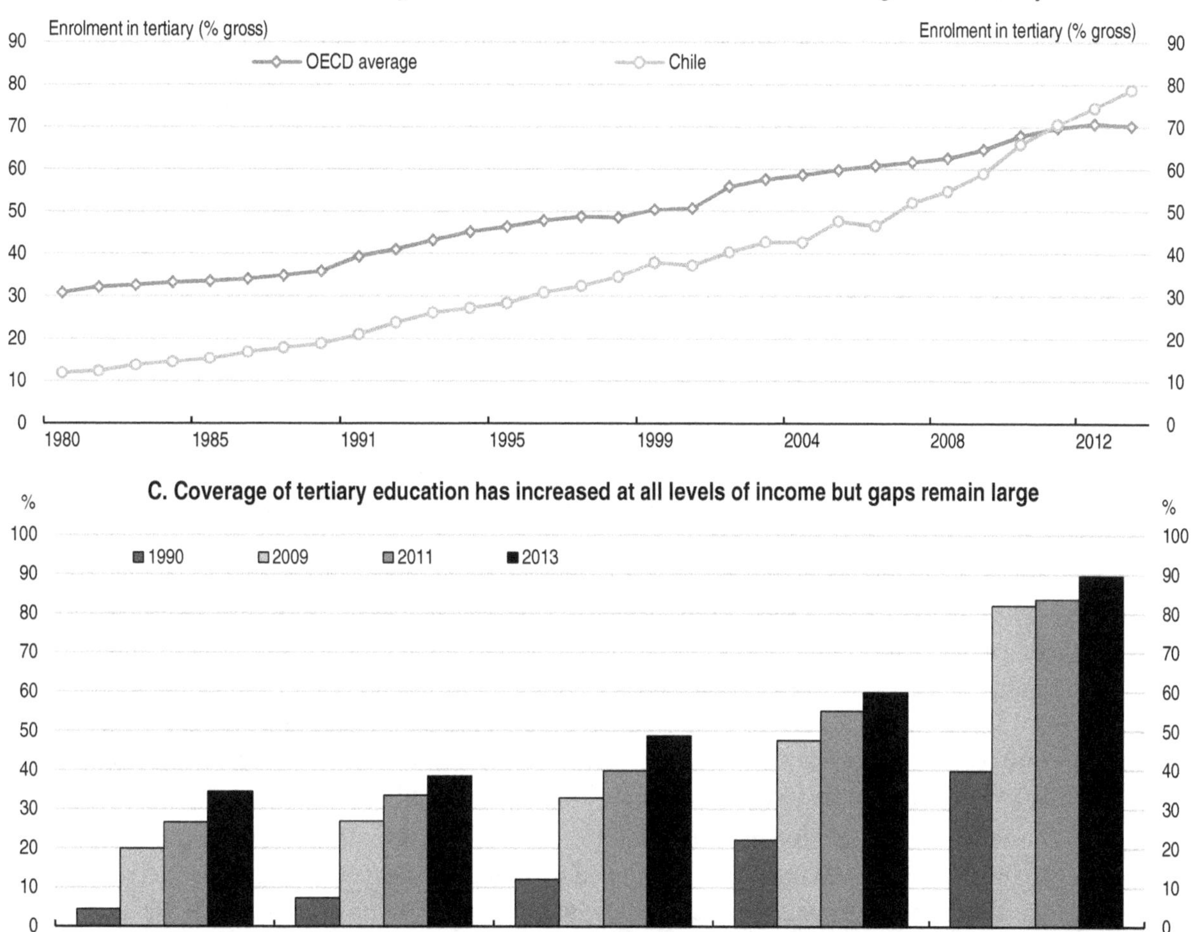

Note: "Gross enrolment" in Panel B is the ratio of students of all ages that attend tertiary education and students within the official age group. Thus, if there is late or early enrolment, or repetition, the total enrolment can exceed the population of the age group that officially corresponds to the level of education – leading to ratios greater than 100%.

Source: Panels A and C: OECD elaboration based on CASEN (1990, 2009, 2011 and 2013). Panel B: World Development Indicators.

StatLink http://dx.doi.org/10.1787/888933302289

If enacted, the bill will imply a significant cost for the fiscal accounts. To solve this problem, a less costly solution could be to offer income-contingent loans to finance tuition fees rather than free education (Dearden, Fitzsimons and Wyness, 2011). Income-contingent loans are also more equitable and satisfy more fully the ability-to-pay principle, because graduates' payments are in direct proportion to their income. Such systems can achieve a better balance between effective cost recovery on the government side and risk to the borrower. Furthermore, under these schemes administration is generally simpler and cheaper because loan recovery can be handled through existing collection mechanism, such as the income tax administration or the social security system. In any case, Chile should develop a funding system for tertiary education that, like in other OECD countries, ensures equal access and strong labour market outcomes for all (Box 2.1). A funding system that better links education to current and future labour market needs, and provides incentives to enhance quality.

Furthermore, free education does not guarantee students from lower income families will have access to, and will be able to graduate from, tertiary education. Some countries at similar level of development as Chile provide free tertiary education for all, but have lower levels of enrolment of students from low income families than Chile. For example, while in Chile a student from the wealthiest quintile of the income distribution is four times more likely to be enrolled in tertiary education than a student from the lowest quintile, in Argentina is five times despite the fact that it provides free education for all (UNESCO-IESALC, 2008). This is because the most important constraints to access tertiary education for students from low socio-economic backgrounds are non-financial. Evidence from other countries shows that low high school quality, as well as insufficient parental involvement, pose greater obstacles to access (and graduate from) university than financial constraints (Frenette, 2007).

Tackle horizontal inequality

Resolving financial barrier constraints will not alone solve inequality challenges. In addition to "vertical inequality", the Chilean higher education system is also characterised by "horizontal inequality", which relates to the kind of institutions and programmes students attend and determine subsequent labour market opportunities (Salmi and Basset, 2012). Some groups of the population are systematically tracked into categories of institutions and programmes that are less resourced or recognised in terms of labour market rewards (Figure 2.11). This is because the strong inequalities remaining in the school system translate to inequalities in the access to high-quality tertiary education. Chances to enter high-quality universities and access to financial aid for them are very much dependent on results at a university PSU entry exam. And not surprisingly given PISA and SIMCE results, PSU exam results are strongly dependent on family income and the school type that pupils attended, with the highest failure rates among low-income pupils.

Therefore, as discussed before, the key for Chile is first to improve the quality and equity of pre-primary, primary and secondary education to achieve universal skills; but this will take time. The government needs to take steps to hold schools accountable for the results of their pupils in the university entry exam, and to improve the preparation of low-income students. The government will need to intervene in those schools where it identifies shortcomings. More immediately, the government will have to find means to better help young people with university aspirations at disadvantaged schools to prepare for the university entry test. A good starting point would be to expand the offering of free

Box 2.1. Funding systems for universities: Three OECD examples

Providing sufficient and stable resources to tertiary education and ensuring equal access and strong outcomes are central policy objectives in most countries. However, the approach followed to reach these goals varies considerably. This box presents three very different examples.

In the United States, states have a large experience with public performance-based funding. Historically, grants were mainly allocated according to indicators of final outcomes with labour market outcomes playing a large role. But the role of labour market outcomes in funding has recently been downplayed due to the impact of the economic downturn. Now in some states (e.g. Ohio), public funding is only allocated according to the number of courses and degrees completed by students. The allocation of grants also attempts to ease access of students from disadvantaged backgrounds. In Tennessee for instance, institutions are eligible to a 40% bonus for completion of low-income and adult students. Around half of university funding comes from tuition fees, which have been increasing since 1990. Overall public and private expenditure per student in tertiary education was in 2012 the highest in the OECD, contributing to the high quality of some US universities. Government sponsored student loans enable students from disadvantaged backgrounds to finance tertiary education. However, this funding system has led to increasing student debt as well as to loan defaults with the economic downturn. These trends have had consequences for public finances as the government provides guarantees and in some cases pays interest for less advantaged students.

In France, two *Grandes Écoles, Sciences-Po* Paris and *Université Paris Dauphine*, have introduced tuition fees tied to the student's parental income or the student's own income, if he/she is independent from his/her parents (Mangeol, 2014). The purpose of the approach is to increase resources and ensure social equity. For example, in Sciences-Po the fees for an undergraduate degree range from zero for students from lower socio-economic backgrounds to EUR 9 940 for those from upper socio-economic families, with 11 different brackets. This approach remains highly contentious in France. It could lead to the polarisation of universities between affluent and constrained institutions, since the resources generated highly depend on the socio-economic composition of the student body.

In Denmark, higher education is mostly publically funded through grants determined by the so-called "taximeter" system and without tuition fees. In addition, students receive student grants to cover their living costs. Taximeter "rates" are set by the government to the activity of institutions – measured by the number of students who have completed the programme – according to various criteria, including the field of education, political priorities, teachers' salaries and building and administrative costs. *Ex post* however, institutions are free to allocate the grant as they wish and can move funds from one area to another. The system gives institutions incentives to adjust their capacity to demand and to raise efficiency, and it ensures that resources are automatically transferred from programmes with declining activity to those with rising activity. However, the system does not provide incentives to students to choose an education programme or a field of study according to its labour market outcomes. To strengthen the quality of higher education, in 2014, the government decided to try to limit the intake of education programmes that have led to relatively bad labour market outcomes. If, over the last 10 years, a group of related education programmes has had an unemployment rate for graduates (after two years) that is more than 2 percentage points above the average unemployment rate for graduates in at least seven of the years, the student intake of programmes in the group will be adjusted. The number of places in this group of programmes will be lowered by 10 to 30% depending on the size of the unemployment gap for graduates.

Source: OECD (2015g), *OECD Skills Outlook 2015: Youth, Skills and Employability.*

Figure 2.11. **There are large horizontal inequalities in higher education**

A. Enrolment by type of institution is highly correlated with family income

■ 2-year degree □ 4-year degree ■ 5-year degree: Public ■ 5-year degree: Private □ Not enrolled

%

100 90 80 70 60 50 40 30 20 10 0

0-556 557-1,668 1,669-2,800 2,801-3,900 >3,900

Family income (USD per month)

B. Average monthly earnings vary a lot by degree type, 2010

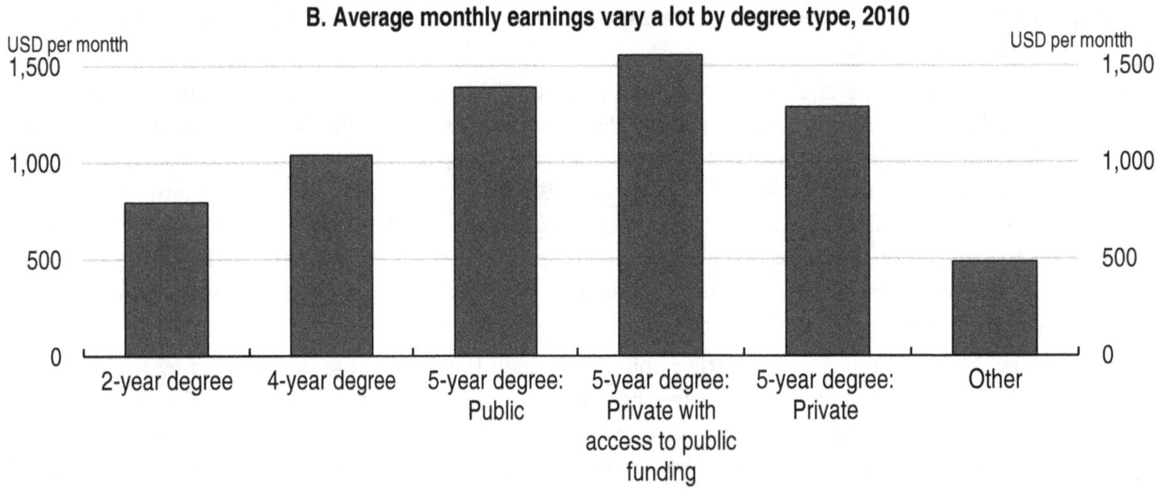

Source: Reyes and Urzua (2013).

StatLink http://dx.doi.org/10.1787/888933302565

online open courses to prepare for the exam. But over time the government should consider replacing the university entry exam with a national school leaving exam as the prime criterion for entry into tertiary education institutions. This could establish a closer link between test results and the school that is responsible for them, making it easier to reach the goal that has been pursued with the introduction of the PSU.

Finally, many students in Chile express *ex post* regret over excessive student loan debt relative to their earnings potential. One possible explanation is that some students base educational choices on limited or inaccurate information on the costs and benefits of studying different subjects. This suggests a role for government in aggregating and disseminating information and indicates that informational interventions alone may not ensure that students make efficient choices about educational investments. The high level of university drop-outs reflects failures in the guidance process as well as poor programme quality and high cost of education (Rau et al., 2013; OECD, 2008). Career guidance should provide a full picture of the various pathways in the education system. Guidance in vocational education and training has an important role to play in supporting individuals to identify how they can best use the skills they have developed through their course of education and training to build fulfilling careers. More efforts can be dedicated to providing individuals and families with timely, relevant information on the market returns of various career paths, and on appropriate education and training programmes that have been monitored to ensure quality.

Activating skills and using them effectively

For skills to translate into growth, they have to be efficiently allocated and used in the economy. However, the degree of qualification mismatch is higher in Chile than in many OECD countries (Randstad Workmonitor, 2012). Recent research shows that skill mismatch can explain an important share of cross-country labour productivity gaps (Adalet McGowan and Andrews, 2015). Skills mismatch is a complex challenge that requires a whole-of-government approach to ensure that product and labour markets are sufficiently flexible to enable skills to be used effectively across the economy. In Chile, one factor contributing to the high level of skill mismatch may be that young people do not leave the education system with the skills that employers want and need to enhance productivity. This could be the result of low-quality tertiary programmes and/or a lack of links with the labour market. But it can also be because universities are reluctant to teach skills aimed specifically at employability, as that may lower their academic standards and objectives (Lowden et al., 2011).

Preparing people for the labour markets requires education systems that are flexible and responsive to the needs of the labour market, and young people having access to high-quality career guidance and further education that can help them to match their skills to prospective jobs. But employers also need to become actively engaged in both designing and providing education programmes, and that institutional obstacles to entering the labour market, even for those with the right skills, are removed. Creating these conditions requires a concerted effort by education providers, the labour market, social institutions, and employer and employee organisations. To improve in this regard, Chile should develop a national qualification framework to ensure that it reflects labour-market relevant skills, to make it easier for young people to clearly signal what skills they possess to employers and to facilitate recruitment processes.

Strengthen vocational education and training to better respond to labour market needs

University is not the only route to pursue further education. An alternative way to prepare students for the labour market is through vocational education and training (VET), both at upper-secondary and postsecondary level. Across the OECD, there are many examples of vocational education and training systems that work very well (Box 2.2). Strong VET systems, such as in Austria, Germany and Switzerland, provide young people with the vocational skills needed for a smooth school-to-work transition, can help engage those who have become disaffected with academic education, and offer higher level-job specific training to adults at postsecondary level (Quintini and Manfredi, 2009). The Chilean VET system provides learning opportunities in remote regions, support for students at risk, labour market integration programmes, and up-skilling for older workers. However, compared to other OECD countries, Chile's VET system remains relatively small. About one third of all upper-secondary students enrol in vocational programmes while two

Box 2.2. Examples of vocational education and training systems in the OECD

Vocational education and training (VET) programmes vary across OECD countries in how they are linked to workplace training and how they establish bridges with other pathways within the educational system. This box provides a few examples.

In the Netherlands, the schooling system is characterised by a high degree of early streaming. However, the different learning routes – including vocational programmes – are structured in such a way that young people have the possibility to go up a step within the track they have chosen, and reach the equivalent of tertiary level education (ISCED 5 level). Possibilities for upstream transfers also exist between vocational and university education.

In Germany access to university for VET graduates was formally enhanced in 2009 and is strongly supported by government campaigns. The new regulations permit those with an advanced vocational qualification general access to academic higher education and holders of other vocational qualifications a subject-specific access to higher education. To support those pursuing this pathway a range of measures have been piloted or rolled out nationally and initiated locally such as advancement scholarships or bilateral credit transfer systems between individual vocational colleges and universities of applied science. Yet, implementation remains a challenge, as it crucially hinges upon the collaboration between individual institutions. In Germany, social partners are closely engaged in the development and updating of training plans for each qualification, which are formally issued by the thematically involved federal ministry (e.g. economy, health) in accordance with the Ministry of Education. Such training plans regulate the duration of the workplace training, describe the profile of the profession, and set out final exam requirements. Apprenticeship salaries are determined through collective wage negotiations. The chambers of commerce advise participating companies, register apprenticeship contracts, examine the suitability of training firms and trainers, and set up and grade final exams.

In Switzerland, the involvement of professional organisations (trade and employer organisations and trade unions) in VET policy making is required by law. Professional organisations draft the core curricula and have the leading role in the examination process of both secondary and post-secondary programmes. The role of Swiss authorities (at Confederation level) is to approve the curricula and examination rules, supervise examinations and issue federal diplomas. When new federal diploma qualifications are approved, they are industry-led, but the federal authorities check that the proposed qualification has the support of the whole industry sector, not just some enterprises. This ensures that the whole industry sector can be engaged in the updating of the qualification in response to changes in technology or industry organisation.

Source: OECD (2015g), *OECD Skills Outlook 2015: Youth, Skills and Employability*.

thirds enter general programmes (Kis and Field, 2009). Contrary to most other OECD countries, Chile allocates fewer resources per upper secondary student to vocational programmes than to the general education track (OECD, 2008). In Chile's VET system, quality standards, teacher training, the link between curricula and industry needs, students' literacy and numeracy skills, and workbased learning need to be improved (Caldera Sánchez, 2014; Kis and Field, 2009).

The fact that the result of Chile's fifteen year-olds in reading, mathematics and science remain among the lowest in OECD countries is likely to be a particular problem among VET students, because those with weak numeracy and literacy skills are often directed to the vocational track. According to the OECD review of Chile's VET system (Kis and Field, 2009), upper-secondary VET provides inadequate basic skills preparation for postsecondary programmes that many students aspire to enter (VET Commission, 2009). While compulsory school is meant to teach basic skills, both upper- and postsecondary VET programmes need to offer remedial measures to address students' weak literacy and numeracy skills.

There is a strong argument for systematically screening the students' basic skills at the point of entry to VET in order to identify the students in need of literacy and numeracy support. In the United States, for instance, new entrants to post-secondary community colleges are tested and can be referred to developmental education (Kuczera and Field, 2013). International experience shows that support in basic literacy and numeracy skills can help reduce drop-out and improve retention and completion rates in VET (OECD, 2014a). A promising approach to basic skills teaching within VET programmes is to integrate basic skills with vocational content, as illustrated by the postsecondary Integrated Basic Education and Skills Training (I-BEST) programme in Washington State, the United States. The I-BEST programme combines basic skills teaching with professional training in occupations in high demand and yields college credits in order to improve the labour market outcomes of adults with low basic skills. Evaluation shows that I-BEST students earn more credits and are more likely to complete a programme than other comparable, but non-participating students (Jenkins et al., 2010).

It is necessary, but difficult to make VET fit the needs of the labour market. One of the best ways of doing so is to bring learning into the workplace. Work-based learning encompasses a diversity of arrangements including apprenticeships and work placements that form part of formal vocational qualifications (OECD 2014a; OECD, 2010a). When managed effectively, work-based learning delivers benefits for all participants and contributes to better labour market and economic outcomes: it offers a strong learning environment for participants; an assured linkage between the work-based learning offer and labour market skills demands; an effective employment and recruitment tool; a productive benefit for employers; and value for money for public authorities. However, despite its compelling advantages, workplace training is too often neglected in VET programmes.

As noted in the OECD review of Chile's VET system (Kis and Field, 2009) workplace training, as part of VET programmes, is poorly developed and the mechanisms to assure its quality are weak. An assessment by the Chilean Ministry of Education (MINEDUC, 2010) suggested that as many as 40% of upper secondary VET students do not do the mandatory traineeship to receive their degree. In postsecondary education, only some institutions include practical workplace training. The OECD VET review (Kis and Field, 2009) recommended encouraging workplace training in all parts of the VET system and linking it to effective quality standards, so as to ensure that work-based learning components are connected to defined learning outcomes and assessment. Closer co-operation between education institutions and social partners, both at national level within the VET Commission and the National Council for VET and at local level, would help to familiarise employers, the chambers and trade unions with education programmes, ensure better curriculum alignment to labour market requirements and provision of work-based placements of sufficient quantity and quality, and help provide labour market relevant training to vocational teachers.

Postsecondary VET can cater to the needs of young upper secondary graduates providing them with higher level vocational skills, as well as providing adults with learning opportunities later in their careers. Rapid economic and technological changes mean that some workers need to upskill to remain abreast of changing requirements, while others have to reskill entirely (OECD, 2014a). Postsecondary vocational programmes can help adults deepen their technical, trade, professional and management skills, make a sideways career move, or return to work after a period of concentrating on domestic responsibilities. Reaping the full potential benefits of VET requires high quality provision. Achieving this is a challenge in many VET systems, including Chile. In the Chilean VET system quality assurance mechanisms are weak and particularly so in the postsecondary sector (MINEDUC, 2010). Recent OECD work on postsecondary VET highlights three key elements that underpin high quality: systematic, quality assured and credit-bearing work-based learning; teachers with strong pedagogical skills and up-to-date industry knowledge and experience; and a programme that ensures sound literacy and numeracy skills alongside occupation-specific skills. In Chile's VET sector, data collection and analysis of education outcomes and skills anticipation exercises could support policy design and programme provision and help make career guidance more effective.

Better labour market institutions can help allocate skills more effectively

Updating and improving labour market institutions in Chile can help smooth the transition from school to work and reduce the degree of skill mismatch. Evidence shows that differences in skill mismatch across countries are associated with differences in the policy environment; in particular, a main factor behind high skills mismatches is the stringency of employment protection legislation (EPL) (Adalet McGowan and Andrews, 2015). A more stringent EPL is associated with higher mismatch amongst youth, since it provides scope to reduce the quality of job-worker matching, which is naturally lower amongst young people due to their lack of experience (Adalet McGowan and Andrews, 2015). On the contrary, a more flexible EPL helps firms adjust their labour force and adapt to rapid technological change.

Empirical research based on longitudinal establishment data shows that in Chile, like in many other OECD countries, there are large and persistent productivity differences among plants or firms producing in the same industries (Bergoeing et al., 2010). A healthy and flexible labour market would allow a process of factor reallocation to take advantage of these productivity differences, significantly contributing to aggregate productivity growth. However, in Chile, because of high severance payments, it is harder to reallocate skills and workers towards the most productive sectors. Indeed, estimates show that the aggregate effects of labour misallocation in Chile are significant: If half of the employees in the first quintile of plants' labour productivity distribution were reallocated to the top quintile plants, manufacturing productivity would increase by about 17% (Micco and Repetto, 2012).

As discussed in Chapter 1, current labour market institutions influence outcomes by protecting insiders, while structurally weakening labour demand for women and youth. The asymmetry between job-protection provisions that make it costly to firms to convert fixed-term contracts into permanent contracts should be eliminated or reduced (Figure 2.12). As many youth enter the labour market on temporary contracts, an important issue is to ensure that these temporary jobs act as "stepping stones" into more stable employment and do not trap them in precarious situations with higher risks of becoming unemployed. Empirical evidence suggests that facilitating labour market access through temporary contracts does not help youth's labour market prospects (OECD, 2014b).

Figure 2.12. **Employment protection legislation is relatively more restrictive for permanent workers**

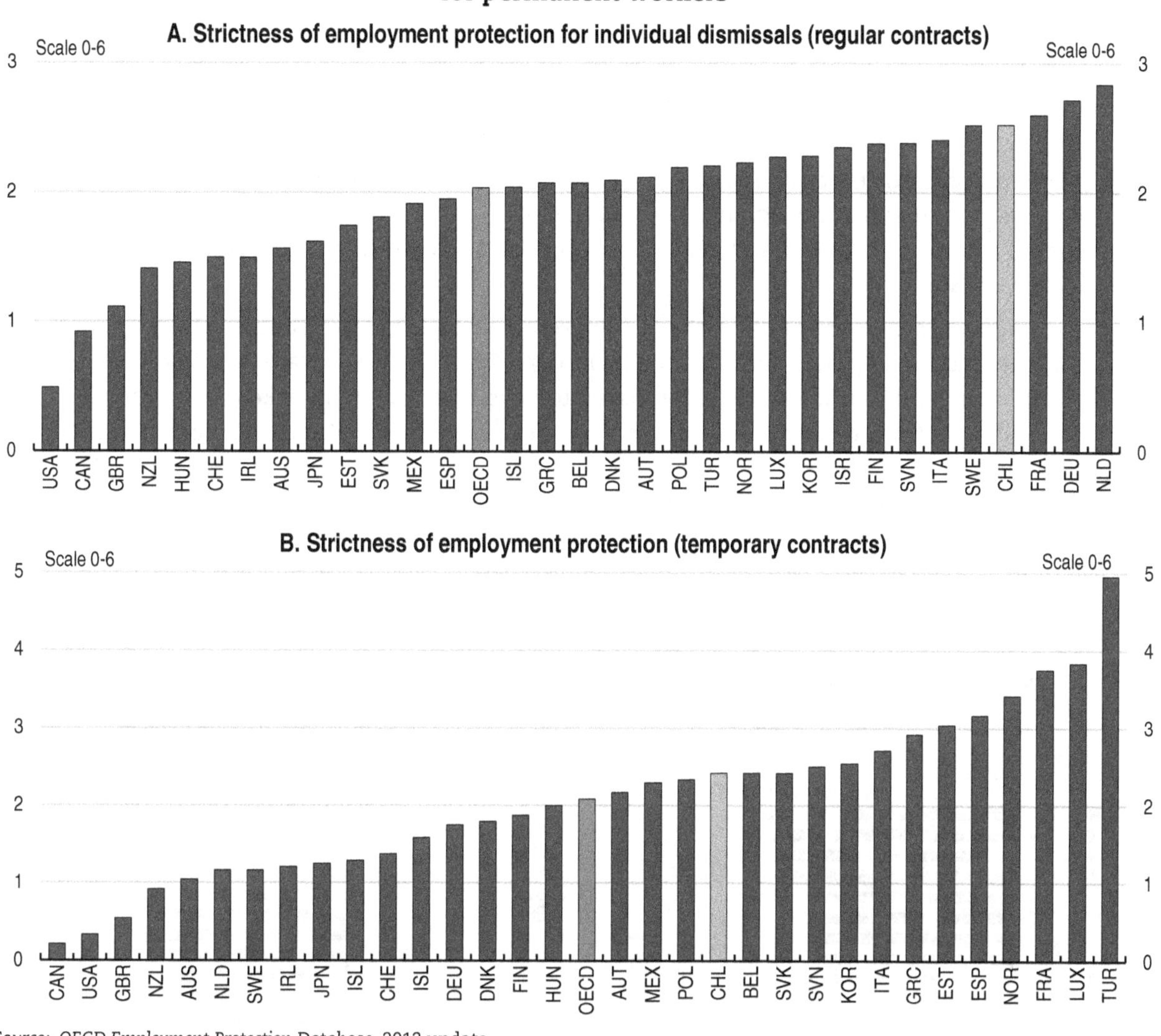

Source: *OECD Employment Protection Database*, 2013 update.

StatLink http://dx.doi.org/10.1787/888933302570

Various policy options have been recently explored in OECD countries to reduce the asymmetry in EPL between temporary contracts and permanent ones. Several countries with a tradition of relatively high levels of protection have taken steps to make termination costs and obligations for different contracts, converging towards a uniform rate or procedure. Italy, for example, has introduced a new open-ended single contract in March 2015, as part of the Jobs Act, a package of labour market reforms introduced by the Renzi administration. This new contract increases employment protection with the job tenure, aiming at simplifying and streamlining dismissal rules while reducing labour market dualism. This new contract is applied only to new employment contracts, grandfathering existing rights. The temporary contracts will be transformed into open-ended ones by 2016, unless collective agreements set flexibility criteria for the use of temporary contracts. As evidence becomes available about the benefits of single contracts, Chile could follow this example which will not only contribute to reducing income inequality (Chapter 1), but also help reduce skill mismatch and boost productivity growth.

Promote more participation of women in the fields of engineering and computer sciences

Lack of advanced human capital, in particular in key science, technology and engineering management (STEM) fields, is a main obstacle to productivity improvements for Chilean firms (OECD, 2013b; OECD, 2013c). One way to start solving this problem is to promote more women participation in these fields. In Chile, like in other OECD countries, women are awarded only a small proportion of university degrees in the fields of engineering, manufacturing and construction and computing, although graduates of these fields are in high demand in the labour market and correspondingly are highly paid (OECD, 2015f).

The main determinant of the under-representation of women is the gap in mathematics and science performance (Summers, 2005; National Academy of Sciences, 2006). Girls tend to underachieve compared to boys when they are asked to formulate situations mathematically, translating a word problem into a mathematical expression (Figure 2.13). Boys' strength in science lies in their greater capacity, on average, to apply their knowledge of science to a given situation, to describe or interpret phenomena scientifically and predict changes. On average across OECD countries, boys outperform girls in this specific skill by 15 score points, but the gender gap is particularly large in Chile (34 score points).

Figure 2.13. **Gender gaps in performance in science and mathematics are high**

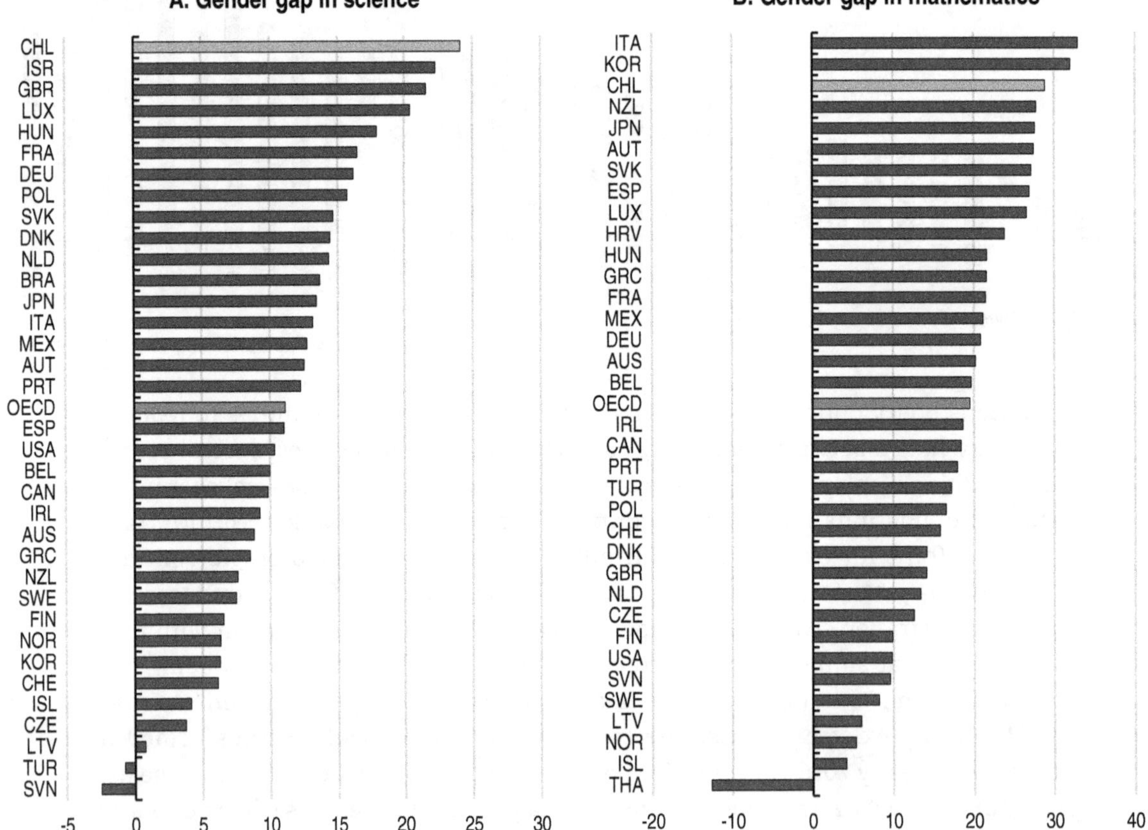

Source: Panel A: OECD, *PISA 2006 Database*. Panel B: OECD, *PISA 2012 Database*.

StatLink http://dx.doi.org/10.1787/888933302589

The fact that fewer women than men enter into careers in science, technology, engineering or mathematics can be related to gender biased stereotypes generated early in life (OECD, 2015f). Evidence shows that parents are more likely to expect their sons, rather than their daughters, to work in science, technology, engineering or mathematics field occupations (Figure 2.14). For example, in Chile, while 50% of 15-year-old boys' parents expected that they would work in science, technology, engineering or mathematics field occupations; only 16% of girls' parents reported so. The gender gap in the percentage of 15-year-old boys and girls whose parents expected them to work in science, technology, engineering or mathematics field occupations is larger than 30 percentage points in Chile.

Figure 2.14. **Parents' expectations for their children careers are gender biased**

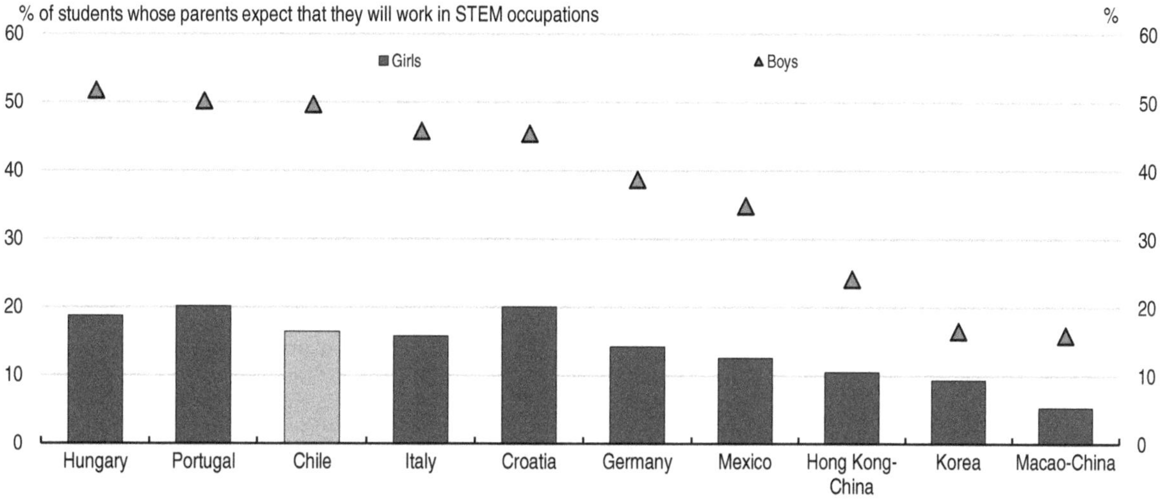

Source: OECD, *PISA 2012 Database.*

StatLink http://dx.doi.org/10.1787/888933302592

When young people choose to pursue a field of study based on someone else's idea of what is appropriate, rather than on their own preference, it is both a waste of individual potential and a loss for society. To reduce gender bias in education Chile should train teachers to be aware of their own gender biases. Teachers may harbour conscious or unconscious stereotyped notions about girls' and boys' strengths and weaknesses in school subjects, and, through the marks they give, reinforce those notions among their students and their students' families. Training teachers to recognise and address any biases they may hold about different groups of students – boys and girls, socio-economically advantaged or disadvantaged students, students from different ethnic or cultural traditions – will help them to become more effective teachers and ensure that all students make the most of their potential.

Recommendations to improve skills

Developing universal basic skills with better quality of education

- Improve the quality and access to pre-primary education.
- Implement legislation to end school selection.
- Increase support to and retention of high quality teachers.
- Make funding responsive to students' and school needs.

Reducing inequalities in access to quality higher education

- Hold schools accountable for their students' university access exams.
- Develop a funding system of universities that better links education to current and future labour market needs, and provides incentives to enhance quality.
- Expand and improve income-contingent loans to finance tuition fees.
- Increase efforts to provide individuals and families with timely, relevant information on the market returns of various career paths, and on appropriate education and training programmes that have been monitored to ensure quality.

Activating skills and using them effectively

- Develop national qualification framework to promote labour market relevance, make it easier for young people to signal clearly what skills they possess, and facilitate recruitment processes.
- Encourage end-of-studies internships within a framework that combines flexibility and obligations to firms.
- Improve both higher education and vocational education and training (VET) programmes by integrating high-quality work-based learning components and ensuring that they also develop cognitive, social and emotional skills.
- Strengthen the co-operation between education and training providers (including universities) and employers.
- Promote women participation in the fields of engineering and computer sciences.

Bibliography

Adalet McGowan, M. and D. Andrews (2015). "Skill Mismatch and Public Policy in OECD Countries", *OECD Economics Department Working Papers*, No. 1210.

Baker, D., B. Goesling and G. LeTendre (2002), "Socioeconomic Status, School Quality, and National Economic Development: A Cross-National Analysis of the 'Heyneman-Loxley Effect' on Mathematics and Science Achievement", *Comparative Education Review*, Vol. 46, No. 3, pp. 291-312.

Barber, M. and M. Mourshed (2007), "How the World's Best-Performing School Systems Come Out on Top", McKinsey & Company, New York.

Bergoeing, R., A. Hernando and A. Repetto (2010), "Market Reforms and Efficiency Gains in Chile", *Estudios de Economía*, Vol. 37, University of Chile, Department of Economics, pp. 217-242.

Brandt, N. (2010), "Chile: Climbing on Giants' Shoulders: Better Schools for all Chilean Children", *OECD Economics Department Working Papers*, No. 784.

Caldera Sánchez, A. (2014), "Policies for Making the Chilean Labour Market More Inclusive", *OECD Economics Department Working Papers*, No. 1117.

Contreras G., D. Ivanov and S. González (2015), "Determinants of early child development in Chile: Health, cognitive and demographic factors", *International Journal of Educational Development*, Vol. 40(2015), pp. 217-230.

Dearden, L., E. Fitzsimons and G. Wyness (2011), "The impact of tuition fees and support on university participation in the UK", *IFS Working Papers*, No. W11/17.

Espinoza, R. and S. Urzua (2014), "Gratuidad de la Educación Superior en Chile en Contexto", *Documento de Trabajo*, No. 4, Centro Latinoamericano de Políticas Económicas y Sociales.

Field, S., M. Kuczera and B. Pont (2007), *No More Failures: Ten Steps to Equity in Education*, Education and Training Policy, OECD Publishing, Paris.

Frenette, M. (2007), "Why are youth from lower-income families less likely to attend university? Evidence from academic abilities, parental influence, and financial constraints", *Analytical Studies Branch Research Paper Series*, Statistics Canada, Ottawa.

Goldin, C. and L.F. Katz (2007), "The Race between Education and Technology: The Evolution of US Educational Wage Differentials, 1890 to 2005", *NBER Working Papers*, No. 12984.

Heckman, J. (2013), "Giving Kids a Fair Chance", *Boston Review of Books*.

Heckman, J.J. and D.V. Masterov (2007), "The Productivity Argument for Investing in Young Children", *Review of Agricultural Economics*, Vol. 29(3), pp. 446-493.

Hsieh, C.T. and M. Urquiola (2006), "The effects of generalized school choice on achievement and stratification: Evidence from Chile's voucher program", *Journal of Public Economics*, Vol. 90(8-9), Elsevier, pp. 1477-1503, September.

ILO (2007), "Skills for improved productivity, employment growth and development", International Labour Conference, 97th Session.

Jenkins, D. et al. (2010), "A Model for Accelerating Academic Success of Community College Remedial English Students: Is the Accelerated Learning Program (ALP) Effective and Affordable?", *CCRC Working Papers*, No. 21.

Kis, V. and S. Field (2009), *OECD Reviews of Vocational Education and Training: A Learning for Jobs Review of Chile 2009*, OECD Reviews of Vocational Education and Training, OECD Publishing, Paris.

Kuczera, M. and S. Field (2013), *A Skills beyond School Review of the United States*, OECD Reviews of Vocational Education and Training, OECD Publishing, Paris.

Lowden, K. et al. (2011), "Employers' perceptions of the employability skills of new graduates", University of Glasgow SCRE Centre and Edge Foundation.

MacLeod, W.B. and M. Urquiola (2009), "Anti-Lemons: School Reputation and Educational Quality", *NBER Working Papers*, No. 15112.

Micco, A. and A. Repetto (2012), "Productivity, misallocation and the labour market", *Documentos de Trabajo 2012*.

MINEDUC (2010), "Educación Técnica Profesional en Chile: Antecedentes y Claves de Diagnóstico", Ministerio de Educación de Chile.

National Academy of Sciences (2006), "Beyond Bias and Barriers: Fulfilling the Potential of Women in Academic Science and Engineering", National Academies Press, Washington, DC.

OECD (2008), *Measuring Improvements in Learning Outcomes: Best Practices to Assess the Value-Added of Schools*, OECD Publishing, Paris.

OECD (2010a), *Learning for Jobs*, OECD Reviews of Vocational Education and Training, OECD Publishing, Paris.

OECD (2010b), *PISA 2009 Results: What Students Know and Can Do – Student Performance in Reading, Mathematics and Science (Volume I)*, PISA, OECD Publishing, Paris.

OECD (2010c), *Educating Teachers for Diversity: Meeting the Challenge*, Educational Research and Innovation, OECD Publishing, Paris.

OECD (2011), *Doing Better for Families*, OECD Publishing, Paris.

OECD (2013a), *How's Life? 2013: Measuring Well-being*, OECD Publishing, Paris.

OECD (2013b), *OECD Science and Technology Scoreboard 2013: Innovation for Growth*, OECD Publishing, Paris.

OECD (2013c), *OECD Economic Surveys: Chile 2013*, OECD Publishing, Paris.

OECD (2014a), *Education at a Glance 2014: OECD Indicators*, OECD Publishing, Paris.

OECD (2014b), *Skills beyond School: Synthesis Report*, OECD Reviews of Vocational Education and Training, OECD Publishing, Paris.

OECD (2015a), *In It Together: Why Less Inequality Benefits All*, OECD Publishing, Paris.

OECD (2015b), *All on Board: Making Inclusive Growth Happen*, OECD Publishing, Paris.

OECD (2015c), *Chile: Policies Priorities for Stronger and more Equitable Growth*, OECD, Paris.

OECD (2015d), *Universal Basic Skills: What Countries Stand to Gain*, OECD Publishing, Paris.

OECD (2015e), *PISA 2012 Results: What Makes Schools Successful (Volume IV) – Resources, Policies and Practices*, OECD Publishing, Paris.

OECD (2015f), *The ABC of Gender Equality in Education Aptitude, Behaviour, Confidence*, PISA, OECD Publishing, Paris.

OECD (2015g), *OECD Skills Outlook 2015: Youth, Skills and Employability*, OECD Publishing, Paris.

Pritchett, L. (2006), "Does learning to add up add up? The returns to schooling in aggregate data", in E.A. Hanushek and F. Welch (eds.), *Handbook of the Economics of Education*, North Holland, Amsterdam, pp. 635-695.

Quintini, G. and T. Manfredi (2009), "Going separate ways? School-to-work transition in the United States and Europe", *OECD Social, Employment and Migration Working Papers*, No. 90.

Randstad Workmonitor (2012). "Skills mismatches and finding the right talent", *Global Report*, No. 3-2012.

Rau, T., E. Rojas and S. Urzua (2013), "Higher Education Dropouts, Access to Credit, and Labor Market Outcomes: Evidence from Chile", mimeo.

Reyes, L., J. Rodríguez and S.S. Urzúa (2013), "Heterogeneous Economic Returns to Postsecondary Degrees: Evidence from Chile", *NBER Working Papers*, No. 18817.

Salmi, J. and R.M. Basset (2012). "Opportunities for all? The equity challenge in tertiary education", *IAU Horizons*, Vol. 17, No. 2, October.

Santiago, P., F. Benavides, C. Danielson, L. Goe and D. Nusche (2013), *Teacher Evaluation in Chile 2013*, OECD Publishing, Paris.

Schleicher, A. (2011), *Building a High-Quality Teaching Profession: Lessons from around the World*, International Summit on the Teaching Profession, OECD Publishing, Paris.

Spinath, B. and F. Spinath (2005), "Development of Self-Perceived Ability in Elementary School: The Role of Parents' Perceptions, Teacher Evaluations, and Intelligence", *Cognitive Development*, Vol. 20, pp. 190-204.

Summers, L.H. (2005), "Remarks at NBER Conference on Diversifying the Science and Engineering Workforce", *www.harvard.edu/president/speeches/summers_2005/nber.php*.

UNESCO-IESALC (2008), "Trends in Higher Education in Latin America and the Caribbean", IESALC, Caracas.

VET Commission (2009), "Executive Summary", *Bases para una política de formación técnico-profesional en Chile (Bases for Vocational Education and Training Policy in Chile)*.

ORGANISATION FOR ECONOMIC CO-OPERATION AND DEVELOPMENT

The OECD is a unique forum where governments work together to address the economic, social and environmental challenges of globalisation. The OECD is also at the forefront of efforts to understand and to help governments respond to new developments and concerns, such as corporate governance, the information economy and the challenges of an ageing population. The Organisation provides a setting where governments can compare policy experiences, seek answers to common problems, identify good practice and work to co-ordinate domestic and international policies.

The OECD member countries are: Australia, Austria, Belgium, Canada, Chile, the Czech Republic, Denmark, Estonia, Finland, France, Germany, Greece, Hungary, Iceland, Ireland, Israel, Italy, Japan, Korea, Luxembourg, Mexico, the Netherlands, New Zealand, Norway, Poland, Portugal, the Slovak Republic, Slovenia, Spain, Sweden, Switzerland, Turkey, the United Kingdom and the United States. The European Union takes part in the work of the OECD.

OECD Publishing disseminates widely the results of the Organisation's statistics gathering and research on economic, social and environmental issues, as well as the conventions, guidelines and standards agreed by its members.

OECD PUBLISHING, 2, rue André-Pascal, 75775 PARIS CEDEX 16
(10 2015 21 1 P) ISBN 978-92-64-24843-4 – 2015

www.ingramcontent.com/pod-product-compliance
Lightning Source LLC
LaVergne TN
LVHW081414110826
845149LV00010B/1747

* 9 7 8 9 2 6 4 2 4 8 4 3 4 *